CREATE IMPRESSIVE + INDULGENT APPETIZER BOARDS
FOR ANY OCCASION

SHARE + SAVOR

KYLIE MAZON-CHAMBERS

Creator of Cooking with Cocktail Rings

PAGE STREET
PUBLISHING CO.

PAGE STREET
PUBLISHING CO.

First published in 2020 by

Page Street Publishing Co.

27 Congress Street, Suite 105

Salem, MA 01970

www.pagestreetpublishing.com

Distributed by Macmillan, sales in Canada by The Canadian Manda Group.

24   23   22   21   20   1 2 3 4 5

ISBN-13: 978-1-64567-013-1

ISBN-10: 1-64567-013-9

Library of Congress Control Number: 2019951591

Cover and book design by Meg Baskis for Page Street Publishing Co.

Photography by Kylie Mazon-Chambers

Printed and bound in China

TO MY GREATEST CHAMPIONS: AARON, MOM, DAD + JOSH

INTRODUCTION

I grew up with a love for entertaining. To this day, I enjoy hosting friends for meals and dinner parties, and not just because, as a food writer, I always have an abundance of food! Although I had a small immediate family growing up, my mom always encouraged an environment where friends were treated like family. We had an open-door policy at our house in suburban New Jersey—it was a safe haven for friends of both my brother's and mine, and the back door was always unlocked. Our friends sometimes stayed for dinner, sometimes for breakfast after a sleepover and sometimes just never left. Any night of the week, we could expect just my mom, dad, brother and me, or it could be a group of ten.

As I started cooking, I quickly learned how to stretch recipes to go far and serve many, or pare down a recipe to serve only a few. I understood the importance of prepping in advance and seeing what elements could be made ahead of time. And most importantly, I learned that food has a way of bringing people together. Whether hosting guests for a casual dinner, apps and drinks or a big holiday party, I've found that one of the easiest ways to please a crowd is with a bountiful charcuterie spread! In this book, I hope to pass along to you my knowledge of creating simple-yet-impressive flavor-forward boards and platters, to help you become a more successful host. Everyone will want to come over every night of the week!

Have you ever noticed at restaurants that sometimes the appetizers and small plates are the most interesting dishes? They have some of the best and most unique flavor combinations! I often end up making a meal entirely of appetizers, or even more frequently, I fill up on appetizers before the entrées arrive. This creativity with flavors is what I wanted to highlight in the boards in this book. Each board gives suggestions for a curated selection of cheeses, cured meats, fruits and/or veggies for a classic spread based on different themes. But to really get that special effect and impress your friends, make the homemade elements! The flavors will blow your mind and perfectly complement the other components in the finished board. Plus, there's flexibility—you can choose to serve these boards either as appetizers or as the meal itself, allowing people to graze as they please.

The spreads and boards in this book are meant to be used as a guide. They can be scaled up for grand parties and gatherings, such as holidays and even weddings, or pared down to their most simple components for a date night for two or an intimate dinner gathering. You can make some of the recipes from the board as stand-alone appetizers or all of them mixed with other elements for an elegant spread—the choice is up to you.

Before making any recipe, don't forget to read it through in its entirety and make a list of everything you need to prevent unnecessary trips to the store (which can be really frustrating right before a party). If you're tackling a larger entertaining board, make a to-do list, breaking down what should be done when. In the board recipes, you'll find that I give a suggested schedule and tips on when different things can be prepped. Of course, these ideas are just a guide, so adapt the plan to fit your own schedule.

Since some parties are more spontaneous, some boards are easier and can be completed with merely a trip to the market, whereas others require a bit of foresight and have multiple components for more of a DIY element. But no matter whether you've never stepped in the kitchen and cooked a day in your life or you're a classically trained chef—there are recipes in here for you.

I love having the ability to share my creations with people, and I am honored to share these recipes with you. I hope they lead to some amazing parties and long nights filled with good food, great conversations and much laughter.

xx,

PART I

CLASSIC ENTERTAINING

The hits, the classics, the all-time favorites with a twist. Over the years, I've made tons of traditional charcuterie boards. But along the way, I began to experiment, adding my own spin on the standards. In this chapter, you'll find my favorite creations curated and crafted to guarantee that guests will be raving about the food at your gathering all year long.

The OG: Classic Cheese and Charcuterie Board (page 11) teaches the basics of how to shop for and organize an elegant and perfectly composed classic cheese and charcuterie board, whereas the Date Night Cheese Board for Two (page 21) focuses on combining make-ahead recipes with store-bought elements for cozy nights in watching an entire season of a TV show. Rather than picking up a premade vegetable tray from the grocery store, opt for a duo of homemade dips with fresh vegetables in the Farmers' Market Crudité Board (page 39). The Assorted Crostini Board (page 27) combines an assortment of toppings on crispy, toasted slices of baguettes, whereas the Fondue Board (page 45) showcases gooey, flavorful cheese with bread and vegetables for dipping.

Whether it's an intimate date night, family picnic or fancy dinner party, I've got you covered for all the classic events.

THE OG: CLASSIC CHEESE AND CHARCUTERIE BOARD

SERVES 10 TO 12

Raspberry-Habanero Jam (page 15)

Cinnamon-Sugar Toast Almonds (page 16)

1 loaf French bread

Baked Brie with Cinnamon and Maple–Roasted Apple (page 19)

8 oz (225 g) Parmigiano-Reggiano cheese

8 oz (225 g) sharp Cheddar cheese

4 oz (115 g) chèvre (goat cheese)

6 oz (170 g) Gorgonzola cheese

4 oz (115 g) prosciutto

4 oz (115 g) sopressata

8 oz (225 g) dry salami, thinly sliced

1 (11-oz [310-g]) piece honeycomb

8 oz (225 g) seedless green grapes

8 oz (225 g) seedless purple grapes

½ cup (71 g) cornichons

2 tbsp (30 ml) whole-grain mustard

1 (4.25-oz [120-g]) box water crackers

1 (2.75-oz [80-g]) box mini toast crackers

This recipe is a foolproof beginner's guide to a great cheese and charcuterie board! A good spread is made of four important elements: cheese, charcuterie, vehicles (crackers and bread) and accoutrements (fresh or dried fruit, nuts and jams) to balance the savory flavors. The most successful boards combine a number of different elements garnished with local and seasonal trimmings. Start by selecting a variety of cheeses. Choose an odd number of both cheeses and charcuterie—either three, five or seven—for the most visually appealing board. Opt for a variety of cheeses with different textures and types of milk (e.g., cow, goat or sheep). Include one familiar cheese on the board, such as Cheddar or Parmesan, to give people a comfortable place to start.

EARLIER IN THE WEEK
Purchase all the ingredients needed for the board. The Raspberry-Habanero Jam can be made and stored for up to 3 months ahead of time. The Cinnamon-Sugar Toast Almonds can be made up to a week in advance.

EARLIER IN THE DAY
Cut the bread into ½-inch (1.3-cm)-thick slices and store them in plastic bags.

1 HOUR BEFORE SERVING
Make the Baked Brie with Cinnamon and Maple–Roasted Apple.

Cheese is best served at room temperature, so take all the cheeses out of the fridge 30 minutes to an hour prior to serving, to let the natural flavors shine.

While the Brie bakes, heat a large grill pan or grill over medium-high heat. Add the slices of bread and cook until grill marks appear, about 1 minute. Flip and cook for an additional minute. Remove and halve the slices on the bias.

Start arranging the cheeses on the board. Separate the different types of cheese into separate areas of the board, arranging any similar style of cheeses opposite each other to show off the variety. To make serving easier, precut any hard cheeses.

(Continued)

THE OG: CLASSIC CHEESE AND CHARCUTERIE BOARD (CONTINUED)

Place the baked Brie on a small plate to keep it contained and then add it to the platter.

Arrange the prosciutto, sopressata and salami around the cheese and fill in the empty spaces with the honeycomb, Cinnamon-Sugar Toast Almonds, grapes and cornichons, using the photo as a reference for placement, if you'd like. Place the jam and the mustard in individual small serving bowls and add them to the platter. Finish with the water crackers, mini toast crackers and grilled bread.

TIP: **When serving a large number of people, bring backup wedges of cheese to replenish the types that are eaten quickly. This gives people a selection and plenty of quantity without overwhelming them. Plan on allotting 2 ounces (55 g) of both cheese and charcuterie per person when serving this board as an appetizer.**

RASPBERRY-HABANERO JAM

MAKES 2 (8-OUNCE [250-ML]) JARS

This sweet and spicy jam pairs well with an assortment of cheeses and charcuterie for a unique accoutrement. The floral, fruity and slightly sour flavors of the raspberry offset the heat and slightly citrus notes of the habaneros. I love it paired with either goat cheese or a hard cheese, such as the sharp Cheddar included on the OG: Classic Cheese and Charcuterie Board (page 11).

As a precautionary measure, I opt to wear gloves or put a plastic bag around my hand to carefully mince the habaneros. If you've had pepper juice on your hands and then accidentally touched your eyes or mouth, it's a mistake to be made only once—the burn of habanero peppers, ranging from 100,000 to 350,000 SHU on the Scoville scale of spice, lingers for quite some time. Lower the number of peppers to only two for a mild heat.

4 cups (500 g) raspberries

3 medium habanero peppers, seeded and minced

3½ cups (700 g) granulated sugar

1 tsp lemon zest

In a medium nonreactive bowl, combine the raspberries, habanero peppers, sugar and lemon zest. Cover with plastic wrap and refrigerate the mixture for at least 1 hour to macerate the raspberries.

Transfer the fruit mixture to a medium pot. Over medium heat, bring the fruit mixture to a rolling boil. Lower the heat to medium-low and simmer, stirring occasionally with a wooden spoon, until the jam is thick but not too concentrated, 45 to 50 minutes. Skim off any foam that rises and discard it.

Divide the jam between two sterilized 8-ounce (250-ml) jars, leaving ¼ inch (6 mm) of space at the top. Close the jars and let them cool to room temperature. Store the jam in the refrigerator for up to 3 months. Serve on the OG: Classic Cheese and Charcuterie Board (page 11) or slathered on bread.

CINNAMON-SUGAR TOAST ALMONDS

SERVES 6 TO 8

These almonds are nostalgic of the cinnamon-sugar toast that my mom used to make for me when I was a kid. For a delicious, sophisticated charcuterie accompaniment, we are combining that familiar taste with roasted almonds. Marcona almonds, a product of Spain, are more rounded and smooth than ordinary almonds and taste like a cross between an almond and a macadamia nut. The sweeter and slightly buttery flavor of the Marcona almonds mixes well with the sweet and warm flavors of the cinnamon for a grown-up snack reminiscent of a childhood favorite. If you can't find Marcona almonds with the other nuts at your local grocery store, check the cheese and deli counter area or a gourmet or natural foods store, such as Whole Foods Market. These cinnamon-sugar-dusted almonds make a great sweet snack to complement the savory cheese and charcuterie of the OG: Classic Cheese and Charcuterie Board (page 11).

1¼ cups (181 g) Marcona almonds

1 tbsp (14 g) unsalted butter, melted

1½ tsp (scant 4 g) ground cinnamon

3 tbsp (39 g) granulated sugar

½ tsp kosher salt

Preheat the oven to 325°F (165°C). In a bowl, toss the almonds with the melted butter and arrange them in a single even layer on an ungreased rimmed baking sheet. Bake, stirring the nuts occasionally, until toasted and golden brown, about 15 minutes. In a small bowl, stir together the cinnamon, sugar and salt. Remove the almonds from the oven and toss with the cinnamon mixture.

Let cool, then store in an airtight container for up to a week. Serve on the OG: Classic Cheese and Charcuterie Board (page 11) or on their own for a sweet snack.

BAKED BRIE WITH CINNAMON AND MAPLE-ROASTED APPLE

SERVES 6

Baked Brie, otherwise known as *Brie en croute*, is one of my favorite appetizers to serve at a dinner party. The flaky, golden brown layers of the puff pastry envelop the melted, bloomy and buttery Brie cheese for a luscious standout feature on a traditional cheese board. Using puff pastry is the classic preparation for this recipe. Not all apples are the same when it comes to baking. I like using Honeycrisp apples because their crisp texture holds when cooked, so you don't end up with a mushy topping. This gooey baked Brie is a great homemade element to contrast the other cheeses on the OG: Classic Cheese and Charcuterie Board (page 11).

1 small Honeycrisp apple (or another crisp, sweet variety), cored and diced

3 tbsp (45 ml) pure maple syrup

1 tbsp packed (15 g) dark brown sugar

1 tsp ground cinnamon

½ cup (60 g) chopped walnuts, divided

8 oz (225 g) frozen puff pastry dough (1 sheet), thawed to room temperature

1 (8-oz [225-g]) wheel double-cream Brie cheese

1 large egg, beaten

In a small bowl, toss the apple with the maple syrup, brown sugar and cinnamon. Transfer the mixture to a medium nonstick sauté pan. Sauté over medium-low heat until the apple is tender and golden brown, about 5 minutes. Stir in ¼ cup (30 g) of the walnuts, then set the mixture aside and let it cool until ready to use. The apple mixture can be made a day in advance and kept refrigerated in an airtight container.

Preheat the oven to 400°F (200°C). Line a baking sheet with parchment paper.

Roll out the puff pastry to a 9 x 12–inch (23 x 30–cm) rectangle. Cut the pastry into a 9-inch (23-cm) circle. Place on the prepared baking sheet and place the Brie wheel in the middle of the pastry. Pile about ½ cup (113 g) of the apple mixture on top. Fold the dough up and over the sides of the cheese, pleating it neatly on top to enclose the cheese and apples. Pinch the dough together to seal.

Brush the pastry with the beaten egg and bake until golden brown, about 35 minutes. Serve immediately, topped with the remaining ¼ cup (30 g) of walnuts. Serve on the OG: Classic Cheese and Charcuterie Board (page 11) or on its own with baguette slices and crackers.

TIP: **To mix it up, try replacing the apple mixture with ½ cup (160 g) of your favorite fruit jam, such classic strawberry or the Raspberry-Habanero Jam (page 15).**

DATE NIGHT CHEESE BOARD FOR TWO

SERVES 2

Champagne Mustard (page 22)

Seeded Rosemary-Fig Crackers (page 25)

8 oz (225 g) seedless red grapes

6 oz (170 g) triple-cream Brie cheese (I like Cowgirl Creamery Red Hawk)

4 oz (115 g) prosciutto or salami

¼ cup (36 g) almonds

This pared-down cheese board needs only one to three cheeses and plenty of wine! Consider this your "Netflix & chill" staple. I like to keep shelf-stable ingredients around to supplement the cheese, so that they can be pulled out at the last minute. Going overboard for just two people can lead to a lot of waste, so opt for simplicity.

The basic way I like to look at this smaller-version cheese board is as a simple formula:

favorite cheese + charcuterie + vehicle + fruit & nut accoutrements = an ideal date night in

For the charcuterie, go for a fan favorite, such as prosciutto or cut salami (both of which can be kept refrigerated for an extended length of time) and for the vehicle, the Seeded Rosemary-Fig Crackers (page 25) or classic water crackers. Whatever fruit you have on hand can be a good substitute for the grapes, if necessary. Figs in season? Grab some of those. Only stocked with apples? Great; cut them up and arrange the slices on the board. The same goes for the nuts. Although I like adding almonds to my cheese board because I typically have them stocked in my pantry, walnuts, pecans or another favorite are good substitutes. While I usually recommend 2 ounces (55 g) of cheese and charcuterie per person, in this case the board is more of a heavy appetizer or in place of dinner, so I opt to increase it to 3 ounces (85 g) of cheese each.

EARLIER IN THE WEEK
Purchase all the ingredients needed for the board. Make the Champagne Mustard; it can be stored in the refrigerator for up to 2 months. Make the Seeded Rosemary-Fig Crackers and store them in an airtight container. Wash the grapes and store refrigerated.

1 HOUR BEFORE SERVING
Remove the cheese from the fridge 30 minutes to an hour before serving and add the mustard to a small bowl. Place the cheese on a plate or board and simply fill in the board with the prosciutto, followed by the mustard, crackers, grapes and almonds, using the photo as a guide for placement, if you'd like.

CHAMPAGNE MUSTARD

MAKES 1 CUP (176 G) OF MUSTARD

While growing up, we used to visit a small sandwich shop that served simple turkey and cheese sandwiches with Champagne mustard, and the mustard turned a relatively lackluster meal into a gourmet treat. After I moved to Los Angeles, I grew nostalgic and started making my own Champagne mustard to add to cheese boards. The Champagne brings a lighter element to usually tangy mustard, and the combination of ground mustard and mustard seeds gives the condiment texture to complement the selection of cheese and meats.

The mustard can be made in advance and stored refrigerated in an airtight container for up to two months and used as needed. This works especially well with the Date Night Cheese Board for Two (page 21) since it can be brought out for impromptu occasions. It complements this board's creamy Brie and salty prosciutto especially well.

⅓ cup (59 g) yellow mustard seeds

¼ cup (36 g) mustard powder

1 tsp kosher salt

½ cup (120 ml) brut Champagne or other dry sparkling wine

¼ cup (60 ml) Champagne vinegar

2 tbsp (30 ml) pure maple syrup

In a small bowl, stir together the mustard seeds, mustard powder and salt. Stir in the Champagne, vinegar and maple syrup; at this point, the mixture will be soupy.

Cover and store at room temperature for 3 days so the mustard seeds absorb some of the liquid and the flavor mellows. Transfer to a blender and pulse until the mixture is thicker but the seeds still have some texture. Transfer to airtight containers and store refrigerated for up to 2 months. Serve on the Date Night Cheese Board for Two (page 21) or with a favorite sliced salami.

TIP: This mustard pairs particularly well with Brie—try serving it with a platter that features Brie, or even on turkey and Brie sandwiches for a lunch or brunch board!

SEEDED ROSEMARY-FIG CRACKERS

MAKES ABOUT 30 CRACKERS

These flavorful homemade crackers are loaded with oats, figs, pumpkin seeds, chia seeds and a bit of fresh rosemary to serve as the perfect vehicle for your favorite cheese, especially when paired with charcuterie and snacks on the simple Date Night Cheese Board for Two (page 21). They taste like healthier Golden Grahams (one of my favorite types of cereal as a kid).

A good cracker should be crisp but not break your teeth. Nothing makes me more self-conscious then taking a bite of an appetizer at a party and fearing that my tooth has cracked. The crackers are first baked as a loaf, then sliced and baked once more to pull some of the moisture out, similar to the method for making biscotti.

1 tbsp (14 g) unsalted butter

1½ cups (188 g) all-purpose flour

½ cup packed (115 g) dark brown sugar

2 tsp (9 g) baking soda

1 tsp kosher salt

1 cup (240 ml) low-fat buttermilk

¼ cup (60 ml) honey

¾ cup (60 g) old-fashioned rolled oats

½ cup (75 g) dried figs, chopped

¼ cup (35 g) pumpkin seeds

2 tsp (7 g) chia seeds

1 tsp chopped fresh rosemary

Preheat the oven to 325°F (165°C). Lightly butter a 1-pound (455-g) loaf pan and line with parchment paper.

In a large bowl or the bowl of a stand mixer, combine the flour, brown sugar, baking soda and salt. Pour in the buttermilk and honey and mix on medium-low speed until incorporated. Add the oats, figs, pumpkin seeds, chia seeds and rosemary and mix on low speed until incorporated. Pour the mixture into the prepared loaf pan and bake until the top is golden brown and a knife inserted at the thickest part comes out clean, about 45 minutes. Meanwhile, line two baking sheets with parchment paper.

Remove the loaf from the oven and transfer it from the pan to a wire rack. Let cool completely, about 30 minutes, then thinly slice the loaf into ⅛-inch (3-mm)-thick slices, about 30 crackers total. Arrange them in a single layer on the prepared baking sheets. Lower the oven temperature to 275°F (135°C) and bake for 15 minutes, then flip the crackers and continue to bake until they are a deep golden brown, an additional 10 to 15 minutes. The crackers may still be a bit tacky but will crisp as they cool.

Remove the crackers from the oven and let cool completely. Store in an airtight container for up to 2 weeks. Serve topped with a favorite cheese or on the Date Night Cheese Board for Two (page 21).

ASSORTED CROSTINI BOARD

There's a restaurant in Phoenix, Arizona, that I love to visit because it has an entire portion of the menu dedicated to mixing and matching various crostini. This board aims to re-create that effect, giving people the option to try various crostini combinations.

When making several different types of crostini, I like to prep all the bread ahead of time. I also cut up all the toppings, set them in separate bowls and place them in the fridge. This makes it easy to assemble mise en place just before serving.

Dinner parties can be a lot of work, so an alternative idea for serving is to set the ingredients as a bar, providing the components in separate bowls and adding a pile of the toasted bread. Be sure to place a list off to the side of the combinations that can be assembled from the ingredients to allow guests a more interactive appetizer board.

EARLIER IN THE WEEK
Purchase all the ingredients needed for making the different crostini recipes. Cut the bread into slices according to the crostini recipes' directions and store in airtight containers until ready to use.

1 DAY BEFORE SERVING
Marinate the pork for the Sliced Gochujang Pork Chop with Peaches and Goat Cheese Crostini. Make the smashed peas for the Smashed Pea and Burrata Crostini; the white beans and the roasted garlic for the White Bean and Roasted Garlic Crostini; and the bacon for the Bacon, Blue Cheese and Fig Crostini. Store these elements in the fridge once they're ready.

(Continued)

ASSORTED CROSTINI BOARD (CONTINUED)

1 TO 2 HOURS BEFORE SERVING

Begin by preparing the crostini slices: The base of all the crostini is the same—sliced bread dipped in olive oil and broiled until crispy. All the bread can be prepared at the same time and topped with the various combinations in each recipe. Preheat your broiler to high. Dip one side of each baguette slice in the olive oil, then arrange the slices, oil side up, on an ungreased baking sheet. Broil just until golden brown, about 2 minutes.

Cook the pork according to its recipe.

Assemble the Bacon, Blue Cheese and Fig Crostini according to their recipe, warming the bacon in a pan if you made it ahead. Assemble the Smashed Pea and Burrata Crostini according to their recipe, warming the smashed peas if you made them ahead. Then, assemble the White Bean and Roasted Garlic Crostini according to their recipe, warming the white beans if you made them ahead. Finish by plating the warm Sliced Gochujang Pork Chop with Peaches and Goat Cheese Crostini according to their recipe, too.

I like to arrange the various types of crostini throughout the board so it is easy for people to reach a variety of toppings. Serve immediately.

SLICED GOCHUJANG PORK CHOP WITH PEACHES AND GOAT CHEESE CROSTINI

SERVES 6 TO 8

Gochujang is a fermented Korean hot pepper paste packed with umami flavor, and it's one of my favorite ways to add spice to a dish. Those with a spice aversion don't need to worry; the sweetness of the fermented soybeans and glutinous rice in the sauce cuts the spice. The marinated spicy pork chops are paired with sweet, juicy, ripe peaches and tart goat cheese for a unique punch of flavor that makes a delicious complement to the other crostini flavors of the Assorted Crostini Board (page 27).

In a small bowl, whisk together the gochujang, sake, soy sauce and garlic. Season the pork chops with salt and pepper, then place in a large plastic bag along with half of the marinade to coat. Refrigerate for at least an hour and up to a day in advance. Set the remaining marinade aside in an airtight container and refrigerate until ready to use.

Remove the pork from the marinade (discard this portion of the marinade), then pat dry and let sit at room temperature for 30 minutes. Heat a 12-inch (30-cm) cast-iron skillet over medium heat, add the vegetable oil and heat through. Sear the pork chops until golden brown on both sides, about 6 minutes total.

Add the reserved marinade to the pan and simmer, lowering the heat to medium-low. Turn the pork chops once. Simmer until cooked through, about 5 minutes total; the internal temperature near the bone should be 135°F (57°C). Transfer the pork chops to a plate to rest for 10 minutes, then slice into ½-inch (1.3-cm)-thick slices.

Directions for batch-cooking the crostini are given in the Assorted Crostini Board recipe (page 27). If making individually, preheat your broiler to high. Dip one side of each baguette slice in the olive oil, then arrange the slices, oil side up, on an ungreased baking sheet. Broil just until golden brown, about 2 minutes.

Spread the goat cheese over the top of each slice of bread, then top with a slice of pork and a slice of peach. Garnish with a sprinkle of flaky salt and serve immediately alone or on the Assorted Crostini Board (page 27).

½ cup (160 g) gochujang paste

½ cup (120 ml) dry sake

2 tbsp (30 ml) soy sauce

3 cloves garlic, minced

2 medium bone-in, 1" (2.5-cm)-thick, center-cut pork chops (about 1 lb [455 g])

Kosher salt and freshly ground black pepper

1 tbsp (15 ml) vegetable oil

1 French baguette, sliced into ½" (1.3-cm)-thick slices (about 15 slices)

¼ cup (60 ml) extra virgin olive oil

8 oz (225 g) goat cheese

2 medium yellow peaches, pitted and sliced

Flaky sea salt, to finish

TIP: The pork can be marinated a day before cooking and can then be cooked a day before serving. If you make it ahead, warm it in the microwave or in the oven for 10 minutes at 350°F (177°C). Although these crostini can also be served cold, I prefer the pork to be sliced and plated just before serving.

SMASHED PEA AND BURRATA CROSTINI

SERVES 6 TO 8

This recipe aims to make use of the ingredients in British "mushy" peas—fresh English peas are smashed with a bit of cream and spread on crostini with creamy burrata and then finished with mint leaves. Although frozen peas could be subbed in this recipe, fresh peas are optimal because of their sweet, delicate flavor. The smashed peas can be made a few days ahead of time, but make sure to reheat them just before assembly, since these crostini should be served warm. The creamy peas and burrata mixture contrasts especially well with the sweet and salty Bacon, Blue Cheese and Fig Crostini (page 36) on the Assorted Crostini Board (page 27).

2 tbsp (28 g) unsalted butter

2 cups (300 g) fresh English peas

⅓ cup (80 ml) heavy cream

Kosher salt and freshly ground black pepper

1 French baguette, sliced into ½" (1.3-cm)-thick slices (about 15 slices)

¼ cup (60 ml) extra-virgin olive oil

8 oz (225 g) burrata cheese

2 tbsp (5 g) chopped fresh mint leaves

Heat a medium sauté pan over medium heat, add the butter and allow it to melt. Add the peas and sauté until tender and bright green, stirring occasionally, 6 to 7 minutes. Stir in the cream and season with salt and pepper to taste. Use a potato masher, the back of a fork or a rubber spatula to lightly mash the peas, so they still retain some of their texture. Simmer until the mixture has thickened, about an additional minute. Remove from the heat and set aside.

Directions for batch-cooking the crostini are given in the Assorted Crostini Board recipe (page 27). If making individually, preheat your broiler to high. Dip one side of each baguette slice in the olive oil, then arrange the slices, oil side up, on an ungreased baking sheet. Broil just until golden brown, about 2 minutes.

Top each slice of bread with a spoonful of the smashed pea mixture and then a small piece of burrata. Garnish with the mint and serve alone or on the Assorted Crostini Board (page 27).

WHITE BEAN AND ROASTED GARLIC CROSTINI

SERVES 6 TO 8

The aromatic combination of freshly roasted garlic cloves and buttery white beans finished with rosemary will keep guests wanting more. Roasting the garlic will make the whole house smell incredible and gives the garlic a velvety, spreadable texture. Although I use canned beans in this recipe to cut down on prep time, dried beans that are soaked and then boiled can be substituted. The white bean mixture and roasted garlic can both be made a few days ahead of time and reheated before assembly. They add an inspired garlicky, creamy variety to the other toasts on the Assorted Crostini Board (page 27).

2 large heads garlic

5 tbsp (75 ml) extra virgin olive oil, divided

2 tbsp (28 g) unsalted butter

1 (15.5-oz [439-g]) can cannellini beans, drained and rinsed

1 tsp chopped fresh rosemary

2 tbsp (30 ml) water

¼ cup (25 g) grated Parmesan cheese

Kosher salt

1 French baguette, sliced into ½" (1.3-cm)-thick slices (about 15 slices)

1 tsp fresh thyme

Preheat the oven to 400°F (200°C). Peel away and discard any excess loose paper from the garlic heads. Trim about ½ inch (1.3 cm) off the top of each head to expose the cloves. Drizzle the garlic heads with 1 tablespoon (15 ml) of the olive oil. Individually wrap each head in aluminum foil and roast in the oven until the garlic cloves are soft when pierced with a knife, about 40 minutes. Remove the garlic from the oven, let cool slightly, then squeeze the garlic from the peels and set aside.

Heat a medium saucepan over medium heat, add the butter and allow it to melt. Add the beans, rosemary and water and cook, stirring occasionally, until the beans are heated but still have texture. Stir in the Parmesan and remove from the heat. Season with salt to taste.

Directions for batch-cooking the crostini are given in the Assorted Crostini Board recipe (page 27). If making individually, preheat your broiler to high. Dip one of the cut sides of each baguette slice in the remaining ¼ cup (60 ml) of olive oil, then arrange the slices, oil side up, on an ungreased baking sheet. Broil just until golden brown, about 2 minutes.

Spread each slice of bread with about a clove's worth of the roasted garlic and top with a spoonful of the beans. Garnish with the fresh thyme and serve alone or on the Assorted Crostini Board (page 27).

BACON, BLUE CHEESE AND FIG CROSTINI

SERVES 6 TO 8

The smokiness and saltiness of crispy bacon complements the bold, sharp flavors of blue cheese and sweet, sticky, rich figs in these crostini. For those who are unsure about blue cheese, opt for a milder blue cheese (they aren't all created equal), such as Gorgonzola or Danish Blue. The bacon can be made a day ahead of time and rewarmed in a nonstick pan just before assembly. For a nice variety of textures and flavors, serve these alongside the other recipes on the Assorted Crostini Board (page 27).

12 oz (340 g) thick-cut applewood-smoked bacon

1 French baguette, sliced into ½" (1.3-cm)-thick slices (about 15 slices)

¼ cup (60 ml) extra-virgin olive oil

10 Black Mission figs, quartered

½ cup (60 g) crumbled blue cheese

Slice the bacon into ½-inch (1.3-cm)-wide strips. Set a large sauté pan over medium heat and add the bacon to the cold pan. Cook until the fat has rendered and the bacon is golden brown and crispy, about 10 minutes. Use a slotted spoon to transfer the bacon to a paper towel–lined plate to drain.

Directions for batch-cooking the crostini are given in the Assorted Crostini Board recipe (page 27). If making individually, preheat your broiler to high. Dip one side of each baguette slice in the olive oil, then arrange the slices, oil side up, on an ungreased baking sheet. Broil just until golden brown, about 2 minutes.

Top each slice of bread with figs, blue cheese and bacon pieces. Serve immediately alone or on the Assorted Crostini Board (page 27).

TIP: If fresh figs are unavailable, try substituting fig jam.

FARMERS' MARKET CRUDITÉ BOARD

SERVES 10 TO 12

Creamy Garlic Pesto Dip (page 40)

Beet-Avocado Lentil Dip with Za'atar (page 43)

2 medium watermelon radishes, thinly sliced

1 bunch French breakfast radishes

1 small head purple cauliflower, cut into florets

1 small head cauliflower, cut into florets

1 small head romanesco, cut into florets

1 large English cucumber, cut into spears

1 bunch petite multicolor carrots

1 bunch broccolini, trimmed

2 cups (130 g) sugar snap peas, strings removed

2 cups (300 g) orange cherry tomatoes

2 small heads endive, leaves separated

I'm spoiled living in Southern California just a few blocks from the Santa Monica Farmers Market. Going to the farmers' market has taught me so much about what fruits and vegetables are in season and when. Since you can get a lot of items in grocery stores year-round, it is helpful to see when ingredients are at their peak and to try out some varieties that aren't typically found in stores. Here, they are served raw and arranged around dips for a colorful crudité board. Each vegetable provides a subtle change in texture and taste that complements the flavorful Beet-Avocado Lentil Dip with Za'atar (page 43) and Creamy Garlic Pesto Dip (page 40). This board is simple without seeming simple—it's great for a girls' night in or book club, since it is packed with a variety of elements for dipping into the flavorful dips.

EARLIER IN THE WEEK

Purchase all the ingredients needed for the board. Make the Creamy Garlic Pesto Dip so the flavor has time to mellow, and store it refrigerated in an airtight container.

1 DAY BEFORE SERVING

Make the Beet-Avocado Lentil Dip with Za'atar 1 day before serving (but not longer than that, to keep the color bright). Wait to garnish until just before serving. Cut the radishes and store them refrigerated in a bowl of ice water to keep them crisp. Cut the cauliflower, romanesco, cucumber, carrots and broccolini and keep them refrigerated in airtight containers.

1 HOUR BEFORE SERVING

Transfer each dip to a small white bowl (to let the color of the vegetables and dips shine) and arrange them on opposite sides of the board so it looks balanced. Since there are two dips on this board, I like to play with symmetry. Garnish the lentil dip with the za'atar.

Fill in the board with the watermelon radishes, breakfast radishes, sugar snap peas, cauliflower, romanesco, cucumber, tomatoes, carrots, endive and broccolini around the dips, using the photo as a guide, if you'd like. The vegetables look best when they are layered on top of one another, alternating the colors and making the board look bright. This way, as people eat the vegetables, the board still looks full.

CREAMY GARLIC PESTO DIP

MAKES 3 CUPS (780 G) OF DIP

Although this dip—similar to a Lebanese garlic spread—is garlic heavy, the strong flavors are balanced with pine nuts, basil and lemon juice. The dip should be made at least a day ahead of serving so the garlic has time to mellow, but it can be kept refrigerated in an airtight container for up to a month. The large quantities of garlic stabilize the dip and allow it to emulsify with the oil, giving it qualities of mayonnaise but without eggs. Alternating adding the oil and lemon juice when blending helps keep the mixture from breaking. This dip is bold and bright in flavor, which contrasts well with the savory lentil dip, making them the perfect duo to serve together on the Farmers' Market Crudité Board (page 39).

3 heads garlic, cloves only (about 1 cup [136 g] cloves; see tip)

2 tsp (12 g) kosher salt

1½ cups (355 ml) vegetable oil

1 cup (240 ml) extra-virgin olive oil

¼ cup (60 ml) fresh lemon juice

¾ cup packed (18 g) basil leaves

½ cup (70 g) pine nuts

In a food processor fitted with the blade attachment, combine the garlic cloves and salt and pulse until the garlic is finely chopped, turning off the machine and scraping down the sides with a rubber spatula as needed.

With the food processor running, slowly add the vegetable oil and olive oil in a thin stream, ½ cup (120 ml) at a time, through the chute in the lid. After each addition of oil, add 1 tablespoon (15 ml) of the lemon juice, continuing to alternate adding the vegetable oil, olive oil and lemon juice until incorporated. Blend until the mixture is emulsified and smooth. Add the basil and pine nuts and continue to blend until combined.

Transfer to an airtight container and refrigerate for at least 1 day and up to 1 month until ready to serve. Serve with vegetables for dipping or on the Farmers' Market Crudité Board (page 39).

TIPS: This recipe calls for lots of garlic and fresh is absolutely best. To peel a head of garlic quickly, use the heel of your hand to smash the head so the cloves part from the head, then place them in a deep metal bowl. Top with a second similarly sized metal bowl and shake vigorously, for 10 to 20 seconds. The skin should be loose and most cloves should be peeled. To get rid of that potent garlic smell on your fingers, rub your hands on stainless steel.

Try using this instead of mayonnaise on the next sandwich you make, for a flavorful condiment.

BEET-AVOCADO LENTIL DIP WITH ZA'ATAR

SERVES 6 TO 8

I like to hide veggies within snacks any way I can, and this dip gets its bright pink-purple coloring from the addition of roasted beets. The texture of this creamy lentil dip is similar to that of hummus, with an earthy flavor that pairs well with the beets and zesty lemon. The key to a smooth dip is using a ripe avocado and simmering the lentils until they are almost falling apart—anything else may end up chunky when combined. Za'atar is a Middle Eastern spice mix made from sesame seeds, thyme, marjoram and sumac, which adds aroma and texture to this dip. With its beautiful color and unique flavor that pairs with a wide range of vegetables, this dip is a perfect element to serve on the Farmers' Market Crudité Board (page 39).

1 cup (192 g) dried red lentils

½ medium yellow onion, diced

4 cups (1 L) water

2 medium red beets, peeled and quartered

5 tbsp (75 ml) extra virgin olive oil, divided

1 medium Hass avocado, pitted and peeled

1 clove garlic, chopped

3 tbsp (45 ml) fresh lemon juice

Kosher salt

1 tsp za'atar

In a medium saucepan, combine the lentils, onion and water. Bring to a boil over medium-high heat. Lower the heat to medium-low and simmer until the lentils are tender and falling apart, about 25 minutes. Drain and let cool.

Meanwhile, preheat the oven to 400°F (200°C). Toss the beets with 1 tablespoon (15 ml) of the olive oil and place on an ungreased baking sheet. Roast the beets in the oven until very tender, about 20 minutes. Remove from the oven and let cool.

Add the lentils, beets, avocado, garlic, lemon juice and remaining ¼ cup (60 ml) of olive oil to a food processor or blender and process until smooth. Season with salt to taste, then transfer to a bowl and top with the za'atar.

This hummus dip can be made up to a week ahead of time and refrigerated in an airtight container. Serve with vegetables for dipping, or on the Farmers' Market Crudité Board (page 39).

TIP: Take care when cooking with beets; the juices have a habit of staining anything they touch bright pink!

FONDUE BOARD

French bread, cut into 1" (2.5-cm) cubes

Marble rye bread, cut into 1" (2.5-cm) cubes

Pumpernickel bread, cut into 1" (2.5-cm) cubes

6 large carrots, peeled and sliced into sticks

6 ribs celery, sliced into sticks

Traditional Swiss Cheese Fondue (page 46)

Spinach-Artichoke Fondue (page 49)

Roasted Duck Fat Potatoes (page 50)

4 oz (115 g) Genoa salami

4 oz (115 g) Calabrese salami

2 medium Granny Smith apples, cored and cut into chunks

½ cup (71 g) cornichons

6 medium soft pretzels, warmed

Although I enjoy eating melted cheese any time of year, I love making this board for a cozy night in during the frigid winter months. While I was growing up, my mom would throw fondue parties for me and some of my friends. We would set up two fondue pots to offer a variety of options and provide plates filled with things to dip into the hot cheese. It's a fun, interactive way to serve food for kids and adults alike and can make a full dinner or be followed by courses of braised meat. The mellow fontina-based Spinach-Artichoke Fondue (page 49) complements the more pungent Traditional Swiss Cheese Fondue (page 46) on this board for two different yet thoroughly enjoyable options for dipping.

EARLIER IN THE WEEK
Purchase all the ingredients needed for the board. Cut the bread and store it in resealable plastic bags.

1 DAY BEFORE SERVING
Cut the carrots and celery a day in advance and store them refrigerated in resealable plastic bags. Shred all the cheese needed for the Traditional Swiss Cheese Fondue and Spinach-Artichoke Fondue and store it refrigerated in labeled, resealable plastic bags.

1 TO 2 HOURS BEFORE SERVING
Make the Roasted Duck Fat Potatoes and set them aside until ready to serve.

Set up four small pots or two medium fondue pots according to the product instructions. Since the cheese is hot and stringy, I recommend setting these on different parts of the table or using a lazy Susan so people can try the fondue without reaching. Prepare the two fondues according to their recipes and keep warm.

Reheat and arrange the roasted potatoes around the fondue pots. Arrange the Genoa and Calabrese salami on the board. Cut the Granny Smith apples just prior to serving, to prevent them from browning. Fill in around the pots with the apple slices, cornichons, carrots, celery, breads and pretzels. Spread these elements around so that guests can easily reach the elements to dip.

TIP: After a fondue dinner, the Swiss typically serve tea. It's said that this helps keep the cheese from curdling in the stomach—I don't question it; I just do it because it seems that this would make sense.

TRADITIONAL SWISS CHEESE FONDUE

SERVES 6

I studied abroad in Lausanne, Switzerland, for a semester when I was in college at Pepperdine University. One of my favorite places to eat at was a little fondue restaurant in the center of the town. The only problem was that the waitresses were generally mean older ladies, and since most of us couldn't speak French very well, we were always afraid that we were going to get scolded by them. But we kept going back because the fondue was so delicious! This recipe is based on the classic Swiss recipe for fondue. It's made from two firm, bold cheeses with a slightly nutty flavor—Gruyère and Emmentaler. Both cheeses are great for melting, creating a creamy fondue that pairs perfectly with the vegetables and roasted potatoes from the Fondue Board (page 45).

1½ cups (160 g) shredded Gruyère cheese

1 cup (110 g) shredded Emmentaler cheese

2 tbsp (15 g) all-purpose flour

½ cup (120 ml) white wine

2 cloves garlic, chopped

1 tsp fresh lemon juice

¼ tsp freshly grated nutmeg

¼ tsp freshly ground black pepper

2 tbsp (30 ml) brandy

In a medium bowl, toss the Gruyère and Emmentaler cheese in the flour and set aside.

Heat the white wine in a fondue pot or a medium saucepan over medium heat. Stir in the garlic and lemon juice. Slowly add the cheeses, fluffing with a fork to help combine the mixture as it melts and to keep it from burning on the bottom of the pot. Continue to slowly add the cheese until it appears to have the consistency of honey. It should be thick but not clumpy.

Add the nutmeg and pepper. Continue to fluff the cheese with the fork to combine. Pour in the brandy around the edges. Pull the cheese away from the edges of the pot to allow the alcohol to boil out, leaving just the flavor. Stir one last time to give the cheese a good consistency. Keep over low heat. Serve on the Fondue Board (page 45) or with bread and vegetables for dipping.

SPINACH-ARTICHOKE FONDUE

SERVES 6

The spinach and bits of artichoke hearts add texture to the creamy blend of melted cheeses in this fondue. The key is to use a blend of cheeses that melt smoothly. A combination of Butterkäse, fontina and Parmesan is used to complement the lager, added for flavor for a hearty and elevated take on a classic entertaining dip. Butterkäse is the best cheese you've never heard of. It loosely translates from German to "butter cheese" because of its buttery texture that lends itself well to melting. If you can't find it, Havarti is a fine substitute. The tangy and fresh flavor from the spinach and artichokes in this fondue perfectly complements the richer flavors of the Traditional Swiss Cheese Fondue (page 46) when they are paired together on the Fondue Board (page 45).

1 cup (110 g) shredded Butterkäse cheese

1 cup (110 g) shredded fontina cheese

¼ cup (25 g) grated Parmesan cheese

2 tbsp (15 g) all-purpose flour

5 oz (150 ml) lager beer

3 cloves garlic, chopped

9 oz (255 g) chopped, cooked spinach, drained

½ cup (150 g) chopped artichoke hearts

1 tsp hot sauce (I like Tabasco)

Freshly ground black pepper

In a medium bowl, toss the Butterkäse, fontina and Parmesan with the flour to coat and set aside.

Heat the beer in a fondue pot or medium saucepan over medium-low heat until hot but not boiling, then stir in the garlic. Slowly add the cheeses, fluffing with a fork to help combine the mixture as it melts and to keep it from burning on the bottom of the pot.

Stir in the spinach, artichoke hearts and hot sauce and season with pepper to taste. Keep warm over low heat. Serve on the Fondue Board (page 45) or with bread and vegetables for dipping.

ROASTED DUCK FAT POTATOES

SERVES 4 TO 6

Cooking in duck fat gives body and adds a rich, subtle flavor to roasted potatoes throughout the cooking process. These are also roasted with aromatic rosemary, salt and pepper until the outsides are crispy and golden brown. These luxurious potatoes pair perfectly with the melty cheese fondues on the Fondue Board (page 45).

Although duck fat can be bought at most butcher shops or high-end grocery stores, whenever I cook duck breasts or eat duck confit, I save the duck fat (it's like liquid gold) to use later to make these potatoes or cook anything else typically cooked in another oil, for an extra boost of flavor. If unavailable, the duck fat can be replaced by just about any other oil, but I recommend extra virgin olive oil because of its rich flavor.

1½ lbs (680 g) baby potatoes, halved

¼ cup (55 g) duck fat, melted

Kosher salt

Freshly ground black pepper

1 tsp chopped fresh rosemary

Preheat the oven to 450°F (230°C). Place the potatoes in a large pot and cover with water. Bring the water to a boil and cook until the potatoes are just tender, about 20 minutes.

Drain the potatoes and pat completely dry. Toss in the duck fat and arrange in a single even layer on an aluminum foil–lined baking sheet. Season with the salt, pepper and rosemary. Roast until the potatoes are golden brown and crisp, about 30 minutes. Serve alone or for dipping on the Fondue Board (page 45).

TIP: These potatoes also pair well served alongside a nice steak!

PART II

SPECIAL OCCASION BOARDS

Here we focus on entertaining for special occasions, such as holidays and seasonal parties. Hosting Thanksgiving? Make a prefeast board. Throwing a baby shower? Make a board. Having everyone over for a poolside summer soirée? Make a board. Heading to a sporting event? You guessed it—make a board. Food brings family and friends together like nothing else, and the board ideas in this chapter are designed to help create lasting memories of food and fun. Whether you are wanting a hearty appetizer selection for a chilly winter night (page 55), looking for the perfect finger foods for a tea party (page 63), making mini lobster rolls for a poolside gathering (page 77) or putting together a pregame platter for friends on a chilly fall afternoon (page 71), these unique recipes are a perfect fit.

WINTER HOLIDAY BOARD

SERVES 10 TO 12

1 loaf crusty bread, cut into 1" (2.5-cm) slices

1 cup (135 g) sugared cranberries, for garnish (optional; see tip)

Cranberry-Orange Brie Puff Pastry Bites (page 59)

Baked Camembert with Garlic and Rosemary (page 60)

9 oz (255 g) Pecorino Romano cheese, cut into ½" (1.3-cm) pieces

9 oz (255 g) Gorgonzola cheese

4 oz (115 g) Genoa salami

1 (11-oz [310-g]) piece honeycomb

½ cup (71 g) cornichons

½ cup (50 g) candied walnuts

8 oz (225 g) seedless red grapes

1 (2-oz [56-g]) package mini breadsticks

2 medium pomegranates, cut into quarters

2 medium Fuyu persimmons

10 dried oranges slices

Rosemary sprigs, for garnish

The holidays can be a hectic time. In my mind, there is a dichotomy between two versions of the holidays: There's the ideal that exists in my head filled with the clichéd chestnuts roasting over the open fire, sitting fireside with a good book and a glass of wine, swathed in cashmere as if I just stepped out of a Nancy Meyers movie; then there's the more realistic version that I always forget until I've overcommitted to parties and my days are spent hectically rushing around for last-minute gifts in a constant bone-chilling cold. To find a middle ground between these two contradicting visions, I like to make as many lists as I can before the holidays and overplan to be as prepared as possible. I'd recommend doing any holiday food shopping a few days ahead of time and prepping as much as you can.

The buttery bites topped with Brie and fruity orange cranberry jam (page 59) complement the gooey baked Camembert (page 60). Both contrast well with the mix of crumbly cheeses and salty charcuterie I chose for this board. Serve with a few nice bottles of red wine for a warming winter dinner party.

EARLIER IN THE WEEK

Purchase all the ingredients needed for the board. Slice the bread and store it in resealable plastic bags. Make the sugared cranberries for garnish (if using) and store them in resealable plastic bags at room temperature.

1 DAY BEFORE SERVING

Make the Cranberry-Orange Brie Puff Pastry Bites; once cooled, store them in an airtight container at room temperature until ready to serve.

1 HOUR BEFORE SERVING

Make the Baked Camembert with Garlic and Rosemary.

While it bakes, heat a large grill pan or grill over medium-high heat. Add the slices of bread and cook until grill marks appear, about 1 minute. Flip and cook for an additional minute. Remove and halve the slices on the bias.

(Continued)

WINTER HOLIDAY BOARD (CONTINUED)

Reheat the puff pastry bites if desired, then arrange them on a plate or on a corner of the board. I like to use a darker-colored board for a more wintery feel. Arrange the Baked Camembert with Garlic and Rosemary, Pecorino Romano and Gorgonzola on different corners of the board so that guests are drawn to the various areas. Fill in the rest of the board with the salami, honeycomb, cornichons, candied walnuts and grapes, using the photo as a guide, if you'd like.

Position the breadsticks and bread on the outside of the board and then place the pomegranates, sugared cranberries (if using), persimmons and orange slices. Garnish with the rosemary sprigs. Earthy seasonal elements like these add color and dimension. Subtle garnishes with a purpose help the board come alive!

TIP: **To make the sugared cranberries, in a medium saucepan, bring ½ cup (100 g) of granulated sugar and ½ cup (120 ml) of water to a boil until a syrup forms, about 10 minutes. Remove from the heat and add 1 cup (100 g) of fresh cranberries, let them sit in the syrup for 10 minutes, then drain and spread them on a wire rack until they're tacky to the touch, about 1 hour. Roll the cranberries in 1 cup (200 g) of granulated sugar.**

CRANBERRY-ORANGE BRIE PUFF PASTRY BITES

MAKES 40 BITES

The zesty citrus in these bites works well with the tart-sweet flavors of the cranberry and contrasts with the buttery puff pastry layers and melted bloomy Brie. Cranberries are actually one of just a few fruits native to the United States. They are only in season during fall, specifically months ending in "er", so I like to stockpile them. They last in the fridge for about a month and for about a year in the freezer. These buttery, flavorful bites fit well on the Winter Holiday Board (page 55) when combined with nutty cheeses and pungent baked Camembert. This element balances the board perfectly for a wide variety of flavor profiles.

1 tbsp (6 g) orange zest, divided

½ cup (120 ml) fresh orange juice (from about 4 large oranges)

¾ cup (150 g) granulated sugar

2 cups (200 g) fresh or frozen whole cranberries

All-purpose flour, for dusting

1 (1-lb [455-g]) package frozen puff pastry dough, thawed to room temperature

1 large egg

1 tbsp (15 ml) water

9 oz (255 g) Brie cheese, rind removed

In a medium saucepan over medium heat, bring 2 teaspoons (4 g) of the orange zest, the orange juice and sugar to a boil, stirring until the sugar dissolves. Add the cranberries and continue to cook until the cranberries have burst and the mixture has a jam-like consistency, about 10 minutes. Remove the jam from the heat and let cool completely.

On a clean, lightly floured work surface, roll out 1 sheet of puff pastry into a 10 x 14–inch (25 x 36–cm) rectangle. Use a knife to cut the pastry into 20 equal squares. Repeat with the remaining sheet of puff pastry. Arrange the squares in a single layer on two parchment paper–lined baking sheets and place in the freezer for 15 minutes.

Preheat the oven to 425°F (220°C). Remove the pastry squares from the freezer. In a small bowl, beat the egg with the water. Brush the squares of pastry dough with the egg wash. Cut the Brie into slices. Then spoon 1 rounded teaspoon (10 g) of the jam onto the center of each piece of puff pastry. Place a piece of Brie on top of each.

Bake until the puff pastry rises and turns golden brown, about 15 minutes. Garnish with the remaining teaspoon (2 g) of orange zest and serve warm or at room temperature on the Winter Holiday Board (page 55) or on their own.

TIP: To reheat, preheat the oven to 350°F (180°C). Arrange the bites on a baking sheet and bake until warmed, about 6 to 8 minutes.

BAKED CAMEMBERT WITH GARLIC AND ROSEMARY

SERVES 6

Camembert is a rich, soft, creamy French cheese with an earthy scent and a similar texture to Brie but with a stronger flavor. It lends well to baking since it stays somewhat contained within its rind. Its intense, slightly funky flavor complements the garlic, rosemary and maple syrup for an aromatic and enticing winter appetizer. This recipe takes only a few minutes to prep, but the garlic and rosemary can be added a few hours prior to baking. Camembert also stays melted for a longer period of time than a lot of other cheeses, making it a great option for entertaining. This hearty recipe fits well with the seasonal ingredients included in the Winter Holiday Board (page 55). This gooey, melted cheese contrasts nicely with the firm textures of the other cheeses on the board.

1 (9-oz [255-g]) wheel Camembert cheese, in its wooden box

2 cloves garlic, finely sliced

2 tsp (1 g) fresh rosemary leaves

1 tsp extra virgin olive oil

1 tbsp (15 ml) pure maple syrup

Flaky sea salt (such as Maldon Sea Salt Flakes)

Preheat the oven to 350°F (180°C). Remove the Camembert from any plastic wrapping and place it back into the wooden box it came in or another similarly sized shallow baking dish. Use a small, sharp knife to score a crosshatch pattern across the top of the cheese wheel.

Using the knife to make small holes as necessary, carefully push the slices of garlic into the cheese, followed by the rosemary leaves. Drizzle the top with the olive oil and maple syrup. Bake until the cheese is gooey and melted, about 15 minutes. Sprinkle with the flaky sea salt and serve on the Winter Holiday Board (page 55) or with bread and crackers.

ENGLISH HIGH TEA TOWER

SERVES 10 TO 12

Maple Scones (page 64)

Cheese Cookies (page 67)

Cucumber Tea Sandwiches with Herbed Cream Cheese (page 68)

6 crumpets or English muffins

1 (6-oz [170-g]) jar clotted cream

½ cup (112 g) unsalted butter (1 stick), at room temperature

½ cup (160 g) strawberry jam

12 oz (340 g) large strawberries

Handful of fresh mint leaves, for garnish

Earl Grey tea bags

Green tea bags

Jasmine tea bags

This type of elegant spread is perfect for special occasions, such as bridal or baby showers, or fun events such as a Kentucky Derby watch party. Are there any more royal weddings coming up? Serve the elements on a three-tiered stand for an elegant presentation, or use one large board or various small decorative platters. This tower is made up of elements that are a combination of sweet and savory, with dainty Cucumber Tea Sandwiches with Herbed Cream Cheese (page 68) and thin lacy Cheese Cookies (page 67) as well as crumpets or English muffins and homemade Maple Scones (page 64).

The scones and crumpets are best served warm with a slather of butter, clotted cream and jam. Clotted cream (also known as Devonshire cream) is a thick and tangy spread made by indirectly heating cow's milk until the cream layer rises to the top. It's thicker and more luxurious than whipped cream and a staple for afternoon tea.

Serve this tower alongside a few different options for tea with cream and sugar. I like a selection of Earl Grey or English breakfast, green tea or matcha or something on the fruitier or floral side, such as jasmine or hibiscus.

EARLIER IN THE WEEK
Purchase all the ingredients needed for the tower. Make the Maple Scones and Cheese Cookies and store them in airtight containers at room temperature.

1 DAY BEFORE SERVING
Assemble the cucumber tea sandwiches up to a day in advance and refrigerate them on covered platters until ready to serve.

30 MINUTES BEFORE SERVING
Reheat the scones, if desired, on a baking sheet at 300°F (150°C) for 6 to 8 minutes and keep them warm until just before arranging the tower. Boil water for the tea and keep it hot.

Arrange the sandwiches, scones, cookies and crumpets on a three-tiered stand set in the middle of the table. Place the clotted cream, butter and jam in individual small bowls or jars and arrange them in various corners of the board. Fill it in with the strawberries and mint. Serve with your tea of choice.

MAPLE SCONES

The best scones are not too crumbly, not too dry, yet not too moist. It's a tall order, but a good scone should hold up to being slathered with a combination of butter, clotted cream and jam.

Scones remind me of my grandmother—she taught me how to properly eat scones on a family trip to England back in 2001. At this time I was still a picky eater, so I spent the entire trip living off scones, hot chocolate and fries. Although my palate has expanded, thankfully my love for scones has remained, and this is my favorite recipe for them. These buttery, freshly baked scones are a great homemade element to complement the other elements of the English Tea Tower (page 63). Top them with clotted cream and jam for an afternoon tea treat.

3¼ cups (406 g) all-purpose flour, plus more for dusting

¼ cup (50 g) granulated sugar

2 tsp (9 g) baking powder

½ tsp baking soda

½ tsp kosher salt

¼ tsp ground cinnamon

½ cup (112 g) unsalted butter (1 stick), chilled and cut into ½" (1.3-cm) pieces

½ cup (55 g) chopped pecans

2 large eggs, beaten

⅓ cup (80 ml) pure maple syrup

1¼ cups (300 ml) heavy cream, divided

1 tbsp (15 g) demerara sugar

In a medium bowl, whisk together the flour, granulated sugar, baking powder, baking soda, salt and cinnamon. Cut in the cold butter by hand or using a pastry dough blender until the butter becomes a coarse meal with some pea-sized bits. Stir in the pecans.

In another medium bowl, whisk together the eggs, maple syrup and 1 cup (240 ml) of the cream. Add the liquid ingredients to the dry ingredients and stir until the dough holds together and all the ingredients are evenly incorporated.

Turn out the dough onto a parchment paper–lined and lightly floured baking sheet. Divide the dough in half and form each portion into a 5-inch (12.5-cm)-diameter circle about ¾ inch (2 cm) thick. Brush the tops of the circles with the remaining ¼ cup (60 ml) of cream and sprinkle with the demerara sugar.

Use a knife or bench scraper to cut each circle into six equal triangles. Carefully separate the pieces just so they aren't touching. Place the baking sheet in the freezer to chill for 20 minutes.

While the dough chills, preheat the oven to 400°F (200°C). Bake the scones until golden brown, 18 to 20 minutes. Remove from the oven and let cool on a wire rack. Serve warm or at room temperature on their own or as a part of the English Tea Tower (page 63).

TIP: The scones can be made 1 day ahead of time and stored in an airtight container. If made ahead of time, to reheat, place the scones on a baking sheet and pop them into the oven at 300°F (150°C) for 6 to 8 minutes.

CHEESE COOKIES

MAKES 30 COOKIES

These addictive savory cookies are made from just a few simple ingredients, but are full of flavor. I used to work for a chef who would make something similar. She kept them around for last-minute entertaining, and anytime I would pass through the kitchen, I couldn't help but sneak one. Although these cookies can be made up to two weeks in advance, they also freeze well and can be left at room temperature or quickly warmed in a microwave for ten seconds just prior to serving. These crumbly, savory cookies are the perfect contrast to the sweet scones and cucumber tea sandwiches served on the English Tea Tower (page 63).

1¾ cups (175 g) grated Parmesan cheese

1 cup (225 g) unsalted butter (2 sticks), cut into ½" (1.3-cm) chunks

½ tsp freshly ground black pepper

½ tsp kosher salt

½ tsp dry mustard

¼ tsp cayenne pepper

1½ cups (188 g) all-purpose flour, plus more for dusting

In a food processor fitted with a blade attachment, pulse the Parmesan, butter, pepper, salt, mustard and cayenne until the butter forms small clumps. Add the flour and continue to blend, turning off the machine and scraping down the sides as needed, until a dough forms, about 1 minute.

Turn out the dough onto a clean, lightly floured work surface and knead the dough until it comes together, adding additional flour if needed. Divide the dough in half and press each into a disk. Place each half in between two sheets of waxed paper and roll each into a ¼-inch (6-mm)-thick rectangle. Freeze until firm, about 20 minutes.

While the dough chills, preheat the oven to 350°F (177°C) and line two baking sheets with parchment paper. Use a 1-inch (2.5-cm) round cookie cutter to cut cookies from the dough and arrange them 1 inch (2.5 cm) apart on the prepared baking sheets. Continue with the remaining dough, freezing and rerolling the leftover dough as needed.

Bake until the cookies are dried and a pale golden brown, 16 to 18 minutes. Remove from the oven and transfer to wire racks to cool. Store the cookies in an airtight container until ready to use. These cookies can be made up to 2 weeks in advance.

Serve as a part of the English Tea Tower (page 63) or on their own as a snack.

CUCUMBER TEA SANDWICHES WITH HERBED CREAM CHEESE

SERVES 6 TO 8

Creamy cucumber sandwiches are the ultimate finger food and a classic accompaniment to afternoon tea, making them an essential element of the English Tea Tower (page 63). The bread is slathered with herbed cream cheese and then filled with sliced crisp cucumbers for a fresh and elegant sandwich. I prefer using English (also known as hothouse) cucumber in this recipe because it has smaller seeds, thinner skin and a slightly sweeter, milder flavor than regular cucumbers. The herbed cream cheese can be made a week in advance and refrigerated in an airtight container. Assemble the sandwiches up to a day in advance and refrigerate on covered platters until ready to serve.

8 oz (225 g) cream cheese, at room temperature

3 tbsp (12 g) chopped fresh flat-leaf parsley

2 tbsp (8 g) chopped fresh dill

16 slices white sandwich bread

1 medium English cucumber, peeled and thinly sliced

6 tbsp (84 g) salted butter, at room temperature

In a small bowl, stir together the cream cheese, parsley and dill until combined. Chill until ready to use.

Spread the cream cheese mixture evenly on one side of 8 of the bread slices, then layer the cucumber slices on top of the cream cheese. Spread the butter on one side of the remaining 8 slices of bread. Close the sandwiches, butter side down.

Trim away the crusts and cut the sandwiches into quarters by cutting on a diagonal and then again on the opposite diagonal. Serve alone or as a part of the English Tea Tower (page 63).

TAILGATING BOARD

Cheesy Jalapeño Corn Dip (page 72)

Sticky Honey Korean Chicken Wings (page 75)

1 medium loaf crusty bread, cut into 1" (2.5-cm) cubes

1 head celery, cut into sticks

3 large carrots, peeled and cut into sticks

1 bunch radishes, halved

½ cup (120 ml) blue cheese dressing

½ cup (120 ml) ranch dressing

8 oz (225 g) sharp Cheddar cheese, cubed

8 oz (225 g) Monterey Jack cheese, cubed

1 (13-oz [369-g]) bag tortilla chips

1 (10-oz [280-g]) box Ritz or similar buttery crackers

1 (16-oz [454-g]) bag pretzel bites (a.k.a. Nibblers)

Football was always on the television in my house in the fall. College game days on Saturday were followed by Sundays filled with NFL games. My mom would make dips and chicken wings for us to snack on while we watched; dips and wings didn't have to be just for the Super Bowl. Sports have a wonderful power to bring people together, as long as they are rooting for the same team, I suppose; but then again, there's nothing wrong with a little friendly competition. My parents have hosted many of my friends and our extended family for weekends filled with an abundance of delicious cheesy and fried finger foods, beer and games. This platter is loaded with game day essentials, such as Cheesy Jalapeño Corn Dip (page 72) and Sticky Honey Korean Chicken Wings (page 75), as well as plenty of carbs for dipping, such as chips, bread and pretzels, and an assortment of vegetables to offset all the cheese.

Serve any and all with ice-cold beers for a guaranteed good time

EARLIER IN THE WEEK

Purchase all the ingredients needed for the board. Make the Cheesy Jalapeño Corn Dip and store it refrigerated in an airtight container until ready to serve. Make the gochujang sauce for the Sticky Honey Korean Chicken Wings and store it refrigerated in an airtight container.

1 DAY BEFORE SERVING

Cut the bread and store it in resealable plastic bags. Cut the celery and carrots and store them refrigerated in airtight containers or plastic bags. Cut the radishes, place them in a bowl of ice water and refrigerate them to keep them crisp. Marinate the chicken wings, but wait to fry them since they are best fried and tossed in the sauce just prior to serving.

1 HOUR BEFORE SERVING

Fry the wings and toss them in the sauce. Reheat the corn dip, then place it in a bowl and set it in a corner of a board. Arrange the wings around or on a separate platter. Place the blue cheese and ranch dressings in individual small condiment bowls and arrange them near the wings for dipping. Arrange the carrots, celery and radishes around the board, alternating the vegetables to diversify the colors, using the photo as a guide, if you'd like. Pile the cheeses into the corners, then fill in any gaps with tortilla chips, crackers, bread and pretzels. If there is not enough room on the board, serve the chips and crackers in bowls on the side.

CHEESY JALAPEÑO CORN DIP

SERVES 10 TO 12

No game day or tailgating board is complete without dip, and this recipe makes entertaining easy. It can be assembled ahead of time and reheated before serving. This creamy dip is loaded with cheese and sweet corn in every bite, for a contrast of textures. Although typically I enjoy cooking with fresh corn on the cob and it would work here, I use canned corn in this recipe because it's available all year long and is a cheap, shelf-stable ingredient that you can keep around for impromptu guests. The cheese makes the corn delicious, and I promise you, nobody will be able to tell the difference. Serve with a big bowl of your favorite tortilla chips!

In a medium skillet over medium heat, cook the bacon until crispy and golden brown, about 8 minutes. Transfer the bacon to a paper towel–lined plate to drain, reserving 3 tablespoons (45 ml) of the fat in the pan and discarding the rest.

Return the pan to medium heat and add the onion. Sauté until tender, about 6 minutes. Add the corn and jalapeños, followed by the cream cheese and sour cream, stirring to combine. Heat until the cream cheese is warmed, about 2 minutes, then stir in the cheese, cooking until completely melted and incorporated, about 5 minutes.

Stir in the cayenne, cooked bacon, half the green onion and half of the cilantro. Serve hot or at room temperature, garnished with the remaining green onion and cilantro, on the Tailgating Board (page 71) or with tortilla chips.

TIP: For a milder dip, try replacing the pickled hot jalapeños with mild.

1 lb (455 g) bacon, thinly sliced widthwise

1 cup (160 g) diced yellow onion

3 (15.25-oz [432-g]) cans sweet corn, drained

¼ cup (34 g) chopped pickled hot jalapeño peppers

1 (8-oz [225-g]) package cream cheese

½ cup (115 g) sour cream

1 cup (115 g) shredded Monterey Jack cheese

1 cup (115 g) shredded mozzarella cheese

½ tsp cayenne pepper

3 green onions, thinly sliced, divided

¼ cup packed (11 g) chopped fresh cilantro, divided

STICKY HONEY KOREAN CHICKEN WINGS

SERVES 4

This recipe is inspired by Korean fried chicken, whereby boneless chicken thighs are fried and tossed either in a sticky, savory sauce or with lots of crispy garlic. The main ingredient in the sauce is gochujang—a sweet and spicy fermented Korean chili paste that can be found in the international condiment section of many grocery stores. In a pinch, the wings can be tossed in another favorite sauce or just eaten plain with flavoring from the garlic and ginger marinade.

Wings are an essential component of any game day tailgating spread. This unique take on the classic is an option guests will go crazy for! The sweet and savory flavor of the sauce on the crispy wings complements the Cheesy Jalapeño Corn Dip (page 72) on the Tailgating Board (page 71). Don't forget to serve the wings with a roll of paper towels or napkins!

Prepare the chicken wings: Separate the chicken wings, if whole, into the drumette, wingette (or flat) and tip. Discard the tips. Place the chicken wings in a large bowl and toss with the garlic, ginger, salt and pepper until combined. Cover and refrigerate for at least 1 hour and up to overnight.

Let the wings sit at room temperature for 30 minutes, then toss with the cornstarch. Meanwhile, pour enough vegetable oil into a large, deep cast-iron pan to reach 1 inch (2.5 cm) up the pan. Heat the oil to 350°F (177°C) and, working in batches, shake off any excess cornstarch and fry the chicken wings, turning occasionally, until golden brown all over and cooked through, 6 to 7 minutes. Transfer to a paper towel–lined plate to drain.

While the wings marinate, prepare the gochujang sauce: In a small saucepan over medium heat, whisk together the gochujang, tomato paste, honey, brown sugar, soy sauce, sesame oil and lime juice until all the ingredients are incorporated and the sugar dissolves, about 5 minutes. Remove from the heat and let cool. The sauce can be made up to a week ahead of time and refrigerated in an airtight container until ready to use.

To serve, reheat the sauce, if necessary, and toss with the freshly fried chicken wings. Serve topped with the sesame seeds and green onions, on their own or on the Tailgating Board (page 71).

CHICKEN WINGS

3 lbs (1.4 kg) chicken wings

6 cloves garlic, minced

1 tbsp (6 g) minced fresh ginger

1 tsp kosher salt

1 tsp freshly ground black pepper

½ cup (63 g) cornstarch

Vegetable oil, for frying

GOCHUJANG SAUCE

¼ cup (60 ml) gochujang

2 tbsp (30 ml) tomato paste

5 tbsp (75 ml) honey

2 tbsp packed (30 g) dark brown sugar

2 tbsp (30 ml) soy sauce

1 tbsp (15 ml) toasted sesame oil

2 tbsp (30 ml) fresh lime juice

TO SERVE

2 tsp (6 g) sesame seeds

2 green onions, thinly sliced

TIP: When frying anything in batches, wait a few minutes in between so the oil can heat back up. This way, everything will cook evenly and for the same amount of time.

SUMMER SEAFOOD PLATTER

1 lb (455 g) cooked snow crab cocktail claws (about 23 claws)

6 cooked king crab legs

Smoked Trout Dip (page 82)

Brown Butter Mini Lobster Rolls (page 85)

1 small loaf sourdough bread, cut on the bias into 1" (2.5-cm) slices

Grilled Oysters with Chipotle-Lime Butter (page 81)

2 lemons, cut into wedges

½ cup (120 ml) cocktail sauce

Hot sauce, such as Tabasco, as needed

¼ cup (60 ml) prepared mignonette sauce (see tip)

12 jumbo blue crabs

Oysters on the half shell

1 (1.75-oz [50-g]) jar caviar

1 lb (455 g) poached jumbo (21/25) shrimp, chilled

20 blini

30 saltine crackers

This elegant spread displays an assortment of seafood perfectly for a day spent with family and friends in the summer sun, lounging pool side with a glass (or several) of chilled rosé. On top of Smoked Trout Dip (page 82), Brown Butter Mini Lobster Rolls (page 85) and Grilled Oysters with Chipotle-Lime Butter (page 81), I love including oysters on the half shell. (Make sure to take the time to teach guests to shuck their own!) I also enjoy shrimp cocktail, luxurious caviar, crab (claws, legs and blue crabs) and an assortment of sauces and garnishes. Serve this platter with some small cocktail forks and claw crackers, so guests can get as much meat out of the crabs as possible— bibs aren't a bad idea, either!

When planning a seafood platter, it is best to get the freshest seafood available. I call ahead to my local seafood market to ensure it has exactly what I want and can set it aside for pickup, or you can order specialty items that the market doesn't always carry. This makes it much easier to plan. If you don't have a great selection of seafood in your area, there are plenty of companies that will deliver fresh seafood on ice directly to you—it's amazing what you can find with a quick Google search these days. It's best to arrange for pickup the morning of, or the day before you serve your seafood platter.

1 DAY BEFORE SERVING

Purchase all the ingredients needed for the board. Since seafood is at its best when it's extremely fresh, purchase those items a day in advance for the best quality (however, you can purchase them 2 days in advance, if needed). Since many snow crab claws and king crab legs come cooked and frozen, defrost them and store refrigerated, if necessary.

Make the Smoked Trout Dip a day in advance (it can be made up to 4 days in advance), and refrigerate, covered, until ready to serve. Chop up the lobster for the Brown Butter Mini Lobster Rolls filling, then cover and refrigerate until ready to make the filling.

Slice the bread and store it in a resealable plastic bag until ready to grill.

(Continued)

SUMMER SEAFOOD PLATTER (CONTINUED)

EARLIER IN THE DAY

Make the lobster filling for the lobster rolls. Make the chipotle-lime butter for the grilled oysters and set it aside until ready to serve. Cut the lemon wedges and prepare the cocktail sauce, hot sauce and mignonette sauce in separate bowls and set them aside.

Bring a large pot of water to a boil over medium-high heat. Add the blue crabs and boil until the shells turn bright orange and they are no longer blue, 8 to 10 minutes. Drain and refrigerate the crabs, covered, until ready to serve.

1 HOUR BEFORE SERVING

Heat a grill over medium-high heat. Add the slices of bread and cook until grill marks appear, about 1 minute. Flip and cook for an additional minute. Remove and halve the slices on the bias. Keep the grill on to make the grilled oysters.

Grill the oysters with their butter drizzled over the top just before guests arrive. Toast the lobster rolls and add their filling. Arrange the trout dip, lobster rolls and grilled oysters around various areas of the board. Serve the fresh oysters on the half shell and the caviar on ice in a large, high-sided bowl (so that as the ice melts, it doesn't spill). Arrange the shrimp on a platter or in a bowl with cocktail sauce. Fill in with the snow crab cocktail claws, cooked blue crab and king crab legs.

Arrange the bread, blini and crackers around the board, followed by the bowl of hot sauce, bowl of mignonette and cut lemon wedges.

TIP: **Mignonette sauce is an essential accompaniment to oysters. I buy it premade anywhere I am buying these types of seafoods. You can typically find it in display cases alongside tartar sauce. It's also very easy to make a homemade version with red wine vinegar infused with minced shallots and fresh tarragon.**

GRILLED OYSTERS WITH CHIPOTLE-LIME BUTTER

MAKES 2 DOZEN OYSTERS

Oysters are shucked on the half shell, then topped with butter mixed with chipotle powder, lime and garlic before being grilled until they are the perfect combination of smoky and tender. Look for medium to large oysters with a deep shell to hold the oyster, its juices and the butter. While Kumamoto oysters can be notoriously difficult to shuck, they are ideal for this dish because of their bowl-like shell. The luscious butter can be prepared ahead of time and melted again just before grilling. With their smoky flavor, these grilled oysters contrast the briny, fresh flavors from the Seafood Platter (page 77).

10 tbsp (140 g) unsalted butter (preferably European)

1 clove garlic, minced

2 tbsp (30 ml) fresh lime juice

1 tsp chipotle chile powder

½ tsp kosher salt

2 dozen assorted oysters, shucked, on the half shell

1 tbsp (3 g) chopped fresh cilantro leaves, for garnish

Heat a medium saucepan over medium-low heat, add the butter and allow it to melt. Stir in the garlic and cook until fragrant, about 30 seconds. Whisk in the lime juice, chipotle chile powder and salt, then remove from the heat.

Heat a charcoal or gas grill to medium-high heat. Place the oysters directly on the grates, shucked side up, and spoon a little of the butter into each oyster. Close the grill and cook the oysters until they curl and bubble around the edges, 3 to 4 minutes. Carefully remove, using metal tongs, and serve hot, garnished with the cilantro. Serve on the Summer Seafood Platter (page 77) or on their own.

SMOKED TROUT DIP

SERVES 6 TO 8

I had my first taste of smoked trout on a family vacation to Alaska, and afterward my brother and I were inspired to smoke ourselves a few of the trout he caught in the local river. Because smoked trout can be a bit dry on its own in comparison to some other varieties of smoked fish, I prefer it mixed into a dip of cream cheese, sour cream and a combination of herbs. The pickled onion and capers on top add an acidity to balance the smoky flavors of the creamy trout dip. This dip pairs well with the fresh shellfish included on the Summer Seafood Platter (page 77). The complex flavors of the creamy dip contrast the simplicity of the cooked crab legs and shrimp.

1 (8-oz [225-g]) package cream cheese, at room temperature

½ cup (115 g) sour cream

1 tbsp (15 ml) fresh lemon juice

12 oz (340 g) smoked trout, skin and bones removed

3 tbsp (9 g) diced fresh chives

1 tbsp (3 g) chopped fresh dill, divided

½ tsp freshly ground black pepper

¼ cup (34 g) pickled red onions

2 tsp (6 g) drained nonpareil capers

In a medium bowl, stir together the cream cheese, sour cream and lemon juice until thoroughly combined, then fold in the smoked trout, chives, 1 teaspoon of the dill and the black pepper. The fish should still have some texture.

Cover the dip and refrigerate until ready to use. The dip can be made up to 4 days in advance.

Serve the dip topped with the remaining 2 teaspoons (2 g) of dill, pickled onions and capers. Enjoy on the Summer Seafood Platter (page 77) or on its own with grilled bread for dipping.

TIP: Look for smoked trout in the refrigerated section of grocery stores, by the smoked salmon and lox.

BROWN BUTTER MINI LOBSTER ROLLS

SERVES 12

Lobster hasn't always been the delicacy that it is today; it used to be considered a poor man's food—it was actually so abundant that it was fed to inmates in prisons in the early colonies in North America. Drop that little tidbit of knowledge into conversation the next time the Summer Seafood Platter (page 77) is served and impress your guests! Nowadays, lobsters are highly sought for their rich and tender meat. My favorite way to eat them is packed into warmed, buttered buns as lobster rolls. This version is a riff on Connecticut-style lobster rolls, served with drawn butter—instead, the butter is browned for a nutty taste complemented by an assortment of herbs.

If you don't live in a place where fresh lobster is easily accessible, be sure to ask when the lobster was flown in. If a lobster is out of the ocean and isn't able to eat, the meat in it will begin to break down and it won't be as good. You can often get lobster shipped directly from Maine, overnighted to you for the freshest product.

The amount of meat in lobsters can vary, so talk to your fishmonger for a recommendation on how much to buy based on what is available. The lobster meat can be steamed (my preferred method of cooking lobster) and chopped a day ahead of time. Combine with the brown butter and herbs just prior to serving, so the butter does not coagulate.

1 cup (225 g) unsalted butter (2 sticks), divided

1 lb (455 g) cooked lobster meat (tails, knuckle and claw meat), chopped

1 medium shallot, diced

2 tbsp (8 g) chopped fresh tarragon

2 tbsp (8 g) chopped fresh flat-leaf parsley

1 tbsp (3 g) chopped fresh chives

Kosher salt and freshly ground black pepper

6 top-sliced New England–style rolls, halved

Heat a medium sauté pan over medium heat, add 10 tablespoons (140 g) of the butter and allow it to melt. Cook the butter, swirling it around the pan occasionally, until it is a toasty brown color and has a nutty aroma, around 5 to 7 minutes. Once this happens, immediately transfer the brown butter to a small bowl.

In a medium bowl, toss together the lobster meat, brown butter, shallot, tarragon, parsley and chives. Season to taste with salt and pepper.

Heat a medium sauté pan over medium-low heat, add the remaining 6 tablespoons (85 g) of butter and allow it to melt. Working in batches, add the buns to the pan and toast on both sides until golden brown, about 2 minutes per side.

Fill each halved bun with a scoop of the lobster salad and serve immediately. Serve on the Summer Seafood Platter (page 77) or on their own.

PART III

INTERNATIONAL MEDITERRANEAN BOARDS

Bring a taste of the Mediterranean straight to your dining room with these unique boards inspired by flavors and food from Italy, Greece, Turkey and Spain. Many meals in these cultures are served in small portions (such as tapas in Spain), which lend themselves to bite-sized appetizers that can also be made into full meals. This chapter includes some really bright, amazing flavors and healthy ingredients that will give you a good introduction to using vibrant spices and new techniques (think: pickling!). Try making some of these recipes with a group of friends. They will have as much fun making the boards as they will eating them.

ITALIAN ANTIPASTI BOARD

10.25 oz (290 g) stick salami, thinly sliced

8 oz (225 g) deli-sliced sopressata

Giardiniera (page 93)

1 loaf ciabatta bread

Whipped Ricotta with Honey, Crispy Garlic and Basil (page 94)

Antipasto Skewers with Pesto Oil (page 97)

8 oz (225 g) burrata cheese

8 oz (225 g) Pecorino Romano, cut into 1" (2.5-cm) chunks

1 (6-oz [170-g]) jar 'nduja

1 cup (100 g) Castelvetrano olives

1 (6.5-oz [184-g]) jar herb-marinated artichoke hearts, drained and halved

½ cup (55 g) oil-packed sun-dried tomatoes

1 (6-oz [170-g]) piece honeycomb

1 (3-oz [85-g]) box Italian breadsticks

¼ cup (60 ml) extra-virgin olive oil

1 tbsp (15 ml) balsamic vinegar

¼ tsp freshly ground black pepper

Basil leaves, for garnish

A traditional Italian meal begins with antipasti—an assortment of meats, cheeses and vegetables—before serving the primi, a first course that is typically a form of pasta, then followed by a main course of meat or fish. The best type of antipasti board combines a variety of different textures and flavors. You get a mix of creamy cheeses, spicy salami and 'nduja (spicy spreadable pork sausage), briny pickled vegetables and sweet honey. When selecting Italian meats and cheeses for such a spread, I like to opt for at least one hard cheese, such as Pecorino Romano in all its salty, crumbly glory, as well as a creamy cheese, such as burrata—similar to mozzarella but with a cream-filled center. Both complement the whipped ricotta dip. The skewers and whipped ricotta can be made up to two days prior to serving.

EARLIER IN THE WEEK
Purchase all the ingredients needed for the board. If you obtain the charcuterie from a deli counter, take all the meat out of the paper it's wrapped in and store it in a resealable plastic bag so it doesn't dry out. Make the Giardiniera and refrigerate until ready to serve (since the pickled vegetables can be made up to a few weeks in advance). Cut the bread into slices on the bias and store in resealable plastic bags at room temperature.

1 DAY BEFORE SERVING
Make the Whipped Ricotta the day before serving (but do not garnish with the basil and garlic yet) and store it refrigerated in an airtight container. Make the pesto for the Antipasto Skewers and store refrigerated in an airtight container. Assemble the skewers (but do not drizzle the pesto over the skewers yet) and refrigerate, tented with plastic wrap until ready to serve.

(Continued)

ITALIAN ANTIPASTI BOARD (CONTINUED)

1 TO 2 HOURS BEFORE SERVING

Place the whipped ricotta in a shallow bowl. Fry the toppings for the ricotta and garnish. Arrange the bowl of whipped ricotta, the burrata and the Pecorino Romano in different areas of the board, using the photo as a guide, if you'd like.

Place the 'nduja in a small bowl and add it to the board with the salami and sopressata, followed by the skewers. Drizzle the skewers with the pesto. Layer the salami, arranging it to draw guests' eyes in a line around the board. Fold the slices of sopressata in half and layer on top of one another.

Preheat the oven to broil. Arrange the bread slices on an ungreased baking sheet. Broil until toasted and golden brown, about 2 minutes.

Arrange the olives, Giardiniera, artichokes, sun-dried tomatoes, honeycomb, toasted bread and breadsticks around the board. Combine the olive oil, balsamic and black pepper in a small, shallow bowl or plate and place it on the board. Garnish the board with basil leaves to add pops of color.

GIARDINIERA

MAKES 2 (16-OUNCE [475-ML]) JARS

My uncle is a chef and one of the people I look up to most when it comes to cooking. Whenever I stop by his house in Orange County, he always has an assortment of homemade snacks ready for me, ranging from homemade sausage and cured meats to these crunchy Italian vegetables pickled in a cider vinegar brine. Although giardiniera is classically made with Italian varieties of peppers, I like to follow my uncle's lead and use serrano peppers with the seeds and ribs cut out for a bright spice.

The briny flavor of these pickled vegetables is the perfect contrast to the Whipped Ricotta with Honey, Crispy Garlic and Basil (page 94) and Antipasto Skewers with Pesto Oil (page 97) on the Italian Antipasti Board (page 89). Since this recipe makes two jars of giardiniera, I like to serve one jar to guests and save the other for snacking, as it lasts for a long time! It also makes a great hostess gift.

4 serrano peppers, halved, seeds and ribs removed

1 small head cauliflower, cut into florets

3 medium carrots, julienned

2 medium ribs celery, julienned

1 large red bell pepper, seeds removed and sliced

2 cups (475 ml) cider vinegar

2 tbsp (24 g) granulated sugar

3 cloves garlic, smashed

2 tsp (4 g) black peppercorns

2 tsp (3 g) red pepper flakes

2 tsp (2 g) dried oregano

1 tsp whole cloves

2 dried bay leaves

2 cups (475 ml) water

Bring a large pot of heavily salted water to a boil. Add the vegetables and cook for 1 minute, then drain and transfer to a bowl of ice water to stop the cooking process. Once the vegetables are cooled, drain and set aside.

In a large saucepan, bring the cider vinegar, sugar, garlic, peppercorns, red pepper flakes, oregano, cloves, bay leaves and water to a boil. Remove from the heat and let cool to room temperature. Remove the bay leaves.

Divide the vegetables between two sterilized 16-ounce (475-ml) Mason jars and top up each with the pickling liquid. Seal the lids and refrigerate until ready to use, at least 2 days and up to a month. Serve alone as a snack or as a part of the Italian Antipasti Board (page 89).

WHIPPED RICOTTA WITH HONEY, CRISPY GARLIC AND BASIL

SERVES 6 TO 8

In this recipe, ricotta is transformed from its usual slightly grainy texture to a smooth and velvety spread in minutes—but guests will think you slaved over the appetizer for hours. I opt to use whole-milk ricotta rather than part skim because it gives it a much creamier texture. The dip is pureed in a food processor and can be made up to two days ahead of time. The garlic and basil topping should be made just before serving, to keep it crispy. Spread the creamy whipped ricotta over slices of grilled bread and pair it with slices of the cured Italian charcuterie from the Italian Antipasti Board (page 89).

1½ cups (375 g) whole-milk ricotta, drained

2 tsp (4 g) lemon zest

3 tbsp (45 ml) honey

¼ cup (60 ml) extra virgin olive oil

4 cloves garlic, sliced

12 small basil leaves

In a food processor fitted with the blade attachment or in a blender, combine the ricotta, lemon zest and honey. Blend until the mixture is smooth, turning off the machine and scraping the sides of the bowl as needed, about 1 minute. Serve immediately or store refrigerated, in an airtight container, until ready to use. The whipped ricotta can be made up to 2 days ahead of time.

Just prior to serving, heat a medium nonstick sauté pan over medium-low heat. Add the oil and heat through. Add the garlic and sauté until golden brown, about 30 seconds. Remove the garlic with a slotted spoon and transfer to a paper towel–lined plate. Return the oil to the heat. Add the basil and fry for a few seconds, until crisp. Transfer to the paper towels to drain. Top the whipped ricotta with the garlic and basil. Serve on the Italian Antipasti Board (page 89) or with grilled bread.

ANTIPASTO SKEWERS WITH PESTO OIL

MAKES 24 SKEWERS

This is a twist on the traditional sweet and salty combination of prosciutto and melon. Cherry tomatoes, cantaloupe, baby mozzarella balls and prosciutto are threaded onto skewers and drizzled with light basil pesto oil for an added punch of flavor. The pesto oil can be made up to a week ahead of time and kept refrigerated in an airtight container. These skewers are a great appetizer for any dinner party featuring Italian food, because the skewers allow for people to hold their food in one hand and their drink in the other—a common happy hour struggle. They are the perfect bite-sized pairing for the selection of meats and cheeses on the Italian Antipasti Board (page 89). The best part about them? They don't require cooking!

Prepare the pesto oil: In a food processor fitted with a blade attachment or a blender, combine all the pesto oil ingredients except the salt, and pulse until the basil is chopped and the sauce is thin. Season to taste with salt and refrigerate in an airtight container for up to 1 week, until ready to use.

Prepare the skewers: Cut 12 bamboo skewers in half. Thread half a cherry tomato on a skewer, followed by one piece each of cantaloupe, prosciutto, mozzarella and basil and then the other half of the cherry tomato. Repeat with the remaining ingredients and skewers. The skewers can be threaded 2 days in advance and kept covered in the refrigerator until ready to serve.

To serve, drizzle the pesto oil over the skewers. Serve as part of the Italian Antipasti Board (page 89) or alone as a snack.

PESTO OIL
½ cup packed (21 g) basil leaves

¼ cup (35 g) pine nuts

2 tbsp (30 ml) fresh lemon juice

1 clove garlic, chopped

½ cup (120 ml) extra-virgin olive oil

Kosher salt

SKEWERS
12 oz (340 g) cherry tomatoes, halved

1 lb (455 g) cantaloupe, cut into 1" (2.5-cm) cubes

4 oz (115 g) sliced prosciutto, torn in half

10 oz (280 g) drained baby mozzarella balls (bocconcini or ciliegine)

¼ cup packed (11 g) basil leaves

GREEK-INSPIRED BOARD

SERVES 10 TO 12

Marinated Feta (page 100)

Sweet and Spicy Tzatziki (page 103)

Spanakopita Bites (page 104)

1 large English cucumber, cut into spears

3 bell peppers, cored and sliced

1 medium head cauliflower, cut into florets

3 large carrots, peeled and cut into sticks

1 cup (100 g) black kalamata olives

10 oz (280 g) tricolor cherry tomatoes

Pita bread, warmed and cut into wedges

Crusty bread, cut into ½" (1.3-cm) slices and grilled

8 oz (225 g) Black Mission figs, halved

2 medium lemons, sliced

Dill sprigs, for garnish

Mint sprigs, for garnish

Years ago, my family took a trip to Greece, where we stayed at a small, family-run bed-and-breakfast on the island of Aegina. After a long, languid day spent at the beach, we would walk back up the hill and gather on a patio overlooking the ocean. We were greeted with a table filled with various appetizers complemented by frosty bottles of Mythos, my favorite Greek beer, and by sparkling glasses waiting to be filled with red wine.

Although in ancient Greece, the soil wasn't fertile enough to promote vegetable growth, they are now widely grown and are a staple of the contemporary Greek diet. Current elements important to Greek cuisine include cheese, olives, lemon juice and yogurt as well as such herbs as oregano, dill and mint. Many Greek restaurants and hosts offer a variety of dips and appetizers for a quick meal. On this platter, you will find a selection of Greek favorites, such as kalamata olives, tangy Marinated Feta (page 100), Sweet and Spicy Tzatziki (page 103) and crumbly savory Spanakopita Bites (page 104). All of these pair well with the fresh crisp vegetables on this vegetarian board.

EARLIER IN THE WEEK
Purchase all the ingredients needed for the board. Make the Marinated Feta and Sweet and Spicy Tzatziki and store them refrigerated in airtight containers until ready to serve. You can also make the Spanakopita Bites and freeze them, if you'd like.

1 DAY BEFORE SERVING
Make the spanakopita (or thaw if made earlier and frozen) and store at room temperature in an airtight container. Cut the cucumber, peppers, cauliflower and carrots and store the vegetables refrigerated in resealable plastic bags.

1 HOUR BEFORE SERVING
Place the olives in a bowl and set it in the middle of a large platter alongside a small bowl for discarding the pits. Place the Marinated Feta in a shallow bowl and the tzatziki in another bowl, then arrange them on opposite sides of the board. Pile the Spanakopita Bites in one area on the platter and fill in the board with the cucumber, tomatoes, peppers, cauliflower, carrots, pita, crusty bread and figs, using the photo as a guide for arranging, if you'd like. Garnish with lemon slices, dill and mint for pops of vibrant green color.

MARINATED FETA

SERVES 6

Briny cubes of feta are marinated in rich olive oil seasoned with garlic and spices. Since the feta will take on the flavor of the olive oil, I would recommend using a decent oil (it doesn't need to be your best drizzling bottle, but still a good one!). The garlic infuses the olive oil and helps take the edge off the sharpness of the tangy feta. Feta cheese is an essential part of any Greek-inspired spread—and this flavor-packed marinated feta adds a delicious contrast of textures to the Greek-Inspired Board (page 99).

2 tsp (4 g) cumin seeds

2 tsp (4 g) coriander seeds

1 tsp black peppercorns

½ tsp red pepper flakes

2 cups (475 ml) extra virgin olive oil

5 cloves garlic, smashed

1 tbsp (3 g) chopped fresh dill

2 tsp (3 g) chopped fresh oregano

1 lb (455 g) feta cheese, cut into ½" (1.3-cm) cubes

In a dry, small nonstick skillet, combine the cumin and coriander seeds, peppercorns and red pepper flakes over medium-low heat and toast, shaking the pan frequently, until the spices are fragrant. Transfer to a small bowl.

In a small saucepan, heat the olive oil and garlic over medium-low heat until fragrant but not browned, about 1 minute. Remove from the heat and let cool completely, about 10 minutes. Then transfer to a medium bowl, add the toasted seed mixture, dill and oregano and stir. Gently stir in the feta. Cover and refrigerate for at least 1 day. The Marinated Feta can be made up to 1 week ahead of time. Serve on the Greek-Inspired Board (page 99), alone with toothpicks or spread on bread.

TIP: This recipe is delicious when spread on warmed pita bread or tossed with juicy tomatoes, cucumber and red onion in a Greek salad.

SWEET AND SPICY TZATZIKI

MAKES 2 CUPS (475 ML) OF TZATZIKI

Tzatziki is one of my favorite Mediterranean dips because it's both versatile and requires few ingredients. I add a touch of honey and Aleppo pepper to the traditional dip to give it a little sweet and spicy flavor, which contrasts with the cool yogurt and crisp cucumber mixture. The creamy dip contrasts particularly well with the Marinated Feta (page 100) and crumbly Spanakopita Bites (page 104) on the Greek-Inspired Board (page 99). It's also delicious on its own with vegetables or slathered on pita, burgers or sandwiches.

To ensure paper-thin slices of cucumber, I shave it with a mandoline on a low setting—this also cuts down on prep time. Draining the cucumber slices before stirring them into the seasoned yogurt keeps the dip thick and creamy.

1½ cups (345 g) plain Greek yogurt

1 tbsp (15 ml) honey

1 tsp lemon zest

2 tsp (2 g) chopped fresh dill

2 tsp (2 g) chopped fresh mint

1 tsp Aleppo pepper flakes

½ medium English cucumber, thinly sliced into half-moons

In a medium bowl, stir together the Greek yogurt, honey, lemon zest, dill, mint and pepper flakes. Pat the cucumber slices dry with paper towels to remove some of the moisture, then stir them into the yogurt mixture. Cover and refrigerate for at least 1 hour before serving.

This dip can be made up to 1 week in advance. Serve with the Greek-Inspired Board (page 99) or with pita bread and vegetables for dipping.

TIP: If Aleppo pepper flakes are unavailable, either ancho chile powder or a mix of equal parts cayenne pepper and paprika can be substituted.

SPANAKOPITA BITES

MAKES 32 SPANAKOPITA BITES

This appetizer is stuffed with a spinach and feta filling. Although sometimes spanakopita is made in large trays and cut into squares like a pie, this version is rolled in phyllo dough, so it is easier to eat as a finger food, making it a perfect pairing for the elements on the Greek-Inspired Board (page 99).

The pastries can be rolled ahead of time, frozen, then baked just before serving. They can even be completely baked a few days ahead of time and reheated just before serving. To reheat, bake for about 10 minutes at 400°F (200°C). I opt to use fresh spinach because it is more vibrant, but in a pinch, frozen spinach can be thawed and drained as a substitute. Drain as much liquid as possible from the spinach so the dough does not get soggy.

Kosher salt

2 lbs (905 g) baby spinach

2 cloves garlic, minced

2 large eggs, lightly beaten

1 cup (150 g) crumbled feta cheese

½ cup (50 g) grated Parmesan cheese

2 tbsp (8 g) chopped fresh dill

3 tbsp (45 ml) fresh lemon juice

Freshly ground black pepper

1 (1-lb [455-g]) package frozen phyllo dough, thawed to room temperature

1 cup (225 g) salted butter (2 sticks), melted

Bring a large pot of salted water to a boil over high heat. Working in batches, stir in the spinach until wilted, 2 to 3 minutes. Drain the mixture through a fine-mesh sieve, pressing to remove any excess liquid. Place the wilted spinach in a food processor fitted with a blade attachment and pulse until finely chopped.

Transfer the spinach to a large bowl, add the garlic, eggs, feta, Parmesan, dill and lemon juice and stir until completely combined and the mixture is thick. Season to taste with salt and pepper.

Line a baking sheet with parchment paper. Gently unfold the sheets of phyllo dough, lay out one sheet on a large cutting board and then brush it with melted butter. Lay another sheet on top of the first and brush again with butter. Repeat two more times until there is a stack of four buttered sheets.

Cut the stack lengthwise into four strips, then in half widthwise so you have eight strips total. Scoop 1 tablespoon (20 g) of the spinach filling and place it 1 inch (2.5 cm) from the bottom of the end of each strip. Fold the bottom right corner over the filing to make a triangle. Continue to fold until you have reached the top of the strip, then brush with butter to close. Continue to form triangles with the remaining phyllo dough and filling until all have been used up. At this point, either freeze the spanakopita or get ready to bake.

Preheat the oven to 375°F (190°C). Arrange the phyllo triangles on a baking sheet. Bake the bites until cooked through and golden brown all over, 50 to 55 minutes. Serve hot or at room temperature with the Greek-Inspired Board (page 99) or on their own.

TURKISH MEZE BOARD

Hummus Topped with Ground Lamb (page 108)

Rice and Beef Dolmas (page 111)

Tabbouleh (page 112)

1 medium head cauliflower, cut into florets

1 medium English cucumber, sliced

Pita bread, warmed and cut into triangles

12 oz (340 g) roasted red peppers, sliced

1 cup (100 g) green olives

4 heads Gem lettuce, leaves separated

1 (6.5-oz [184-g]) jar herb-marinated artichoke hearts, drained and halved

2 medium pomegranates, quartered

8 oz (225 g) Turkish green figs, halved

1 cup (175 g) pitted dates

1 cup (130 g) dried apricots

½ cup (73 g) whole almonds

In the Mediterranean, meze (or mezze) translates to "appetizers" or "snacks." Although they can be served as hors d'oeuvres, these small bites can also be provided as a main course alongside an alcoholic beverage, such as wine, or anise-flavored liqueurs, such as Turkish raki or Lebanese arak—the combination is perfect for grazing and for stimulating conversation. This particular spread is inspired by layers of vibrant Mediterranean flavors. Cumin, coriander, lemon, garlic, parsley and mint provide a contrast of both warming and cooling tastes. This board shines with a variety of contrasting textures, including a mix of fresh vegetables and dried fruit, creamy Hummus Topped with Ground Lamb (page 108), briny Rice and Beef Dolmas (page 111) and herbed Tabbouleh (page 112).

EARLIER IN THE WEEK

Purchase all the ingredients needed for the board. Make the hummus for the Hummus Topped with Ground Lamb (but wait to make the lamb topping) and store it refrigerated in an airtight container until ready to serve.

1 DAY IN ADVANCE

Make the Rice and Beef Dolmas and Tabbouleh and store them refrigerated in airtight containers until ready to use. Marinate the lamb in the spices and store refrigerated. Cut the cauliflower and cucumber and store them refrigerated in resealable plastic bags until ready to use.

1 HOUR BEFORE SERVING

Cook the lamb for the hummus according to the recipe. Meanwhile, arrange the hummus, dolmas and tabbouleh around the board, using the photo as a guide, if you'd like. Arrange the pita bread around the dishes and fill in the board with the red peppers, olives, lettuce, cauliflower, cucumber and artichoke hearts. Follow by arranging the pomegranates, figs, dates, apricots and almonds around the board to alternate the textures of the accoutrements.

HUMMUS TOPPED WITH GROUND LAMB

MAKES 3 CUPS (740 G) OF HUMMUS

Hummus in Arabic translates to "chickpeas," which are the base of this popular dip. In this recipe, I top the hummus with seasoned ground lamb for a flavorful and more filling addition. Baking soda softens chickpeas and helps them cook faster. Don't worry if you see the chickpeas begin to break down as they are cooked—that's exactly what we want!—the hummus will be even creamier and smoother.

The hummus can be made up to a week in advance and kept refrigerated in a container. The lamb can be made up to an hour prior to serving or made a day ahead of time and refrigerated in an airtight container, then reheated. This dish is best served on the Turkish Meze Board (page 107) with an assortment of pita bread and vegetables for dipping. The smooth dip with seasoned lamb topping pairs well with the fresh herbs from the Tabbouleh (page 112) and briny grape leaves of the Rice and Beef Dolmas (page 111) of the board.

Prepare the hummus: In a large bowl, soak the dried chickpeas in cold water overnight. Drain and rinse the chickpeas, then transfer them to a medium saucepan and cover with fresh water. Add the baking soda and bring to a boil over medium-high heat. Cook, uncovered, until the chickpeas are soft, about 1 hour. Drain, discarding any chickpea skins, and set aside.

In a blender, combine the lemon juice, garlic and tahini and blend until a paste forms. With the blender running, slowly add the ice water through the opening in the blender lid until a thin, smooth sauce forms. Add the cooked chickpeas and blend until completely smooth, turning off the machine and scraping down the sides as needed. Season to taste with salt and refrigerate for at least 1 hour until the mixture is chilled. It can be made up to a week ahead of time.

Prepare the ground lamb: In a medium bowl, stir together the cumin, coriander, paprika and salt, then add the lamb and mix, using your hands. Heat a large cast-iron skillet over medium heat, add the olive oil and heat through. Add the lamb and cook until browned all over, about 6 minutes.

To serve, place the hummus in a medium serving bowl and top with the lamb. Serve as a part of the Turkish Meze Board (page 107) or with warmed pita and vegetables.

HUMMUS
1 cup (211 g) dried chickpeas

1 tsp baking soda

2 tbsp (30 ml) fresh lemon juice

2 cloves garlic, grated

½ cup (120 g) sesame tahini

1 cup (240 ml) ice water

Kosher salt

GROUND LAMB
2 tsp (5 g) ground cumin

1 tsp roasted ground coriander

1 tsp paprika

½ tsp kosher salt

8 oz (225 g) ground lamb

2 tbsp (30 ml) extra virgin olive oil

TIP: Although starting with dried chickpeas is the best option, in a pinch they can be replaced with two drained and rinsed 15½-ounce (439-g) cans of chickpeas; just leave out the baking soda if using canned.

RICE AND BEEF DOLMAS

MAKES 30 DOLMAS

The term dolmas translates to "stuffed." Many variations of stuffed grape leaves include ground meat or eggplant, but this version is inspired by a Turkish preparation and stuffed with a seasoned rice mixture. Although fresh grape leaves add a brighter flavor, the most readily available grape leaves are those that come in jars, which can be found among pickled vegetables at most grocery stores. Dolmas are an integral part of the Turkish Meze Board (page 107). The popular stuffed grape leaves pair well with the sweet figs and dried apricots included on the board.

1 (8-oz [225-g]) jar grape leaves, rinsed and drained

3 tbsp (45 ml) extra virgin olive oil

1 medium yellow onion, diced

2 cloves garlic, minced

1 lb (455 g) ground (80/20) beef

Kosher salt and freshly ground black pepper

1 cup (195 g) uncooked long-grain white rice

2¾ cups (650 ml) chicken stock, divided

¼ cup (35 g) pine nuts

2 tbsp (8 g) chopped fresh dill

¼ cup (15 g) chopped fresh flat-leaf parsley

¼ cup (60 ml) fresh lemon juice

Bring a large pot of water to a boil over high heat. Add the grape leaves and cook, stirring gently, until the leaves are pliable, about 2 minutes. Drain the leaves, remove and discard the bottom stems and set aside.

Heat a large, high-sided sauté pan over medium heat, add the olive oil and heat through. Add the onion and sauté until tender and translucent, about 6 minutes. Stir in the garlic and sauté until fragrant, about an additional 30 seconds. Add the beef and cook until browned, about 6 minutes. Season to taste with salt and pepper.

Add the rice and sauté, stirring frequently, until the rice is toasted, about 3 minutes. Add 1¾ cups (410 ml) of the chicken stock and cook, covered, stirring occasionally until the rice is tender and has absorbed all of the liquid but is al dente, about 15 minutes. Stir in the pine nuts, dill and parsley and let cool slightly, about 10 minutes.

Cover the bottom of a 5-quart (5-L) heavy-bottomed pot with 4 grape leaves and place the rest of the leaves on a clean work surface. Working 1 grape leaf at a time, lay the leaf flat and place 1 rounded tablespoon (20 g) of rice filling in the center. Fold the bottom part of the leaf up to cover the filling and pull the right and left sides in, then roll to create a tight cylinder.

Place, seam side down, in the pot and continue with the remaining leaves and filling, placing them in a single even layer. Pour the remaining cup (240 ml) of chicken stock and lemon juice over the top and cover with a plate to keep them submerged. Bring the liquid to a boil over medium heat, then lower the heat to medium-low and simmer until tender, about 20 minutes.

Remove from the heat and serve hot or at room temperature with the Turkish Meze Board (page 107) or on their own.

TABBOULEH

Tabbouleh is made from a combination of chopped herbs, diced vegetables and bulgur, a nutty-flavored whole grain made from cracked wheat that is frequently used in Turkish cuisine. Traditional tabbouleh should have a higher proportion of chopped herbs added to the bulgur. The tabbouleh can be made a day or two in advance and served chilled or at room temperature. When served on the Turkish Meze Board (page 107), the tabbouleh is a flavorful, herby contrast to the Hummus Topped with Ground Lamb (page 108). I like piling both together onto a piece of warmed pita bread.

Rinse the bulgur and place in a medium bowl. Pour 1 cup (240 ml) of boiling water over the bulgur and let stand, covered, for 1 hour. Drain any excess liquid and fluff with a fork.

In a medium bowl, combine the bulgur, cucumber, tomatoes, parsley, mint, green onions, garlic, olive oil, lemon juice and Aleppo pepper flakes. Season to taste with salt. Cover and refrigerate until ready to serve. Serve alone as a side or with the Turkish Meze Board (page 107).

TIP: If Aleppo pepper flakes are unavailable, either ancho chile powder or a mix of equal parts cayenne pepper and paprika can be substituted.

½ cup (70 g) uncooked fine bulgur

½ medium English cucumber, cut into ¼" (6-mm) pieces

1 cup (150 g) cherry tomatoes, halved

1½ cups (90 g) chopped fresh flat-leaf parsley

¼ cup (10 g) chopped fresh mint leaves

2 green onions, thinly sliced

2 cloves garlic, minced

¼ cup (60 ml) extra virgin olive oil

2 tbsp (30 ml) fresh lemon juice

½ tsp Aleppo pepper flakes

Kosher salt

SPANISH TAPAS BOARD

SERVES 10 TO 12

Heirloom Pan con Tomate
(page 119)

Patatas Bravas with Saffron Aioli
(page 120)

9 oz (255 g) Manchego cheese

4 oz (115 g) cured chorizo

4 oz (115 g) Iberico ham

4 oz (115 g) Serrano ham

1 cup (100 g) manzanilla olives

1 cup (175 g) pitted dates

½ cup (160 g) fig jam

1 (2-oz [56-g]) can olive oil–packed
anchovies

½ cup (73 g) Marcona almonds

Oregano sprigs, for garnish

Tapas are small plates of assorted finger foods. This style of serving foods has been popularized at restaurants in recent years—where diners are encouraged to order many smaller dishes for the table so that everyone gets to sample an assortment of flavor combinations. As with any origin story, people are hesitant to declare one single version the definitive one. Nevertheless, the story I most believe about the origins of tapas is that it traces back to as early as the thirteenth century with King Alfonso X of Spain, who could only eat small bites of food and drink when he was ill, thus tapas were born.

The Spanish are notorious for their late dinners, served at around 9:00 p.m. or even later, so tapas may be served earlier in the night to hold guests over. While studying abroad, I once went on a weekend trip to Barcelona with some friends, and we were told to go to Can Paixano, nicknamed La Champagneria—a crowded tapas bar with meat hanging from the ceiling, famous for its cava. We spent the day there ordering plates and plates of cured meats and cheese from the bar. I was introduced to such Spanish specialties as Iberico ham and Serrano ham and buttery Manchego cheese. Classic Spanish favorites, such as Heirloom Pan con Tomate (page 119) and Patatas Bravas with Saffron Aioli (page 120), are served on this board alongside Manchego cheese and charcuterie and supplemented by such snacks as olives, dates, fig jam, anchovies and Spanish Marcona almonds.

EARLIER IN THE WEEK
Shop for all of the ingredients needed for the board.

1 DAY BEFORE SERVING
Prepare the tomato mixture to go over the Heirloom Pan con Tomate and store it refrigerated in an airtight container until ready to use. Cut the potatoes for the Patatas Bravas with Saffron Aioli and refrigerate in a bowl covered with water until ready to cook. Make the aioli for the patatas bravas and store it refrigerated in an airtight container.

(Continued)

SPANISH TAPAS BOARD (CONTINUED)

1 HOUR BEFORE SERVING

Make the patatas bravas and top them with the aioli. Let the cheese, chorizo and Iberico and Serrano ham sit at room temperature for 30 minutes to an hour for the best flavor.

Prepare the Heirloom Pan con Tomate and arrange it in slices on a board. Place the patatas bravas, topped with the saffron aioli, in a serving dish and set in another corner of the board, using the photo as a guide for placement, if you'd like.

Position the Manchego in the middle of the board, then fill in the board with the chorizo and ham. Place the olives, dates and jam in individual small condiment bowls and arrange them around the board. Serve the anchovies in the tin and position it on the board. Fill in the empty space with the Marcona almonds. Arrange the oregano sprigs throughout the board to add texture and color variety to the board.

HEIRLOOM PAN CON TOMATE

SERVES 8 TO 10

This variation of the Spanish favorite, pan con tomate, uses juicy heirloom tomatoes for a luxurious punch. It's like Italian bruschetta's easier cousin. Traditionally, it is made with tomatoes grated onto toasted ciabatta, but I like to add a bit of garlic and vinegar to enhance the natural flavors. I think it is important to buy high-quality ingredients for this recipe, such as heirloom tomatoes, high-quality olive oil and fresh bread. The simple yet flavorful pan con tomate complements the complex savory flavors of the charcuterie on the Spanish Tapas Board (page 115). For an added boost of flavor, pile the slices of pan con tomate with anchovies or thin slices of Manchego.

2 large heirloom tomatoes

1 clove garlic, minced

1 tbsp (15 ml) white wine vinegar

Kosher salt

1 loaf ciabatta bread

3 tbsp (45 ml) extra virgin olive oil

1 tbsp packed (4 g) fresh oregano, chopped

Flaky sea salt

Place a box grater in a large bowl. Grate the tomatoes on the largest holes, so that all that's left over is the tomato skins. Finely chop the tomato skins and add them to the bowl. Stir in the garlic and vinegar, then season to taste with salt. (If the tomatoes were very juicy, drain some of the juice, if necessary.) At this point, the mixture can be covered and refrigerated overnight.

Preheat your broiler to high. Halve the ciabatta loaf lengthwise and cut each half into 2-inch (5-cm)-thick slices. Place, cut side up, on an ungreased baking sheet and drizzle the oil over the bread. Broil, checking frequently, until golden brown, about 3 minutes.

Spoon the tomato mixture onto the slices of bread. Garnish with the oregano and flaky sea salt to taste and serve immediately, alone or on the Spanish Tapas Board (page 115).

PATATAS BRAVAS WITH SAFFRON AIOLI

SERVES 4 TO 6

In this dish, potatoes are deep-fried in spicy olive oil, then coated with tomato pan sauce and topped with garlicky, saffron-infused aioli. While this is like a Spanish take on French fries, the shape of the potatoes is more similar to American home fries. Rather than making the aioli from scratch, mayonnaise is simply dressed up by stirring in lemon juice, a bit of olive oil and garlic, for a shortcut. Patatas bravas are a favorite Spanish appetizer and make the perfect hearty pairing with the intense flavors of the chorizo and oily Iberico ham charcuterie selected for the Spanish Tapas Board (page 115).

Prepare the saffron aioli: In a small bowl, combine the lemon juice and saffron threads and let it sit until the juice turns a golden-orange color, about 15 minutes. In a separate small bowl, whisk together the mayonnaise, olive oil, lemon juice mixture and garlic until completely incorporated. Store in an airtight container until ready to use. The aioli can be made up to a week in advance.

Prepare the patatas bravas: Preheat the oven to 250°F (120°C). Pour enough olive oil into a large cast-iron pan to reach ½ inch (1.3 cm) up the side of the pan, then heat over medium heat. Once the oil is hot, working in batches, add the potatoes and fry until crispy and golden brown on the outside and tender on the inside, about 10 minutes.

As the potatoes are ready, spread on a baking sheet and keep warm in the oven. Remove all but 2 tablespoons (30 ml) of the oil from the pan and return to the heat. Whisk in the flour until it becomes golden brown, about 1 minute, then whisk in the tomato paste, smoked paprika and paprika. Add the beef stock and bring to a simmer. Cook until the sauce is smooth and coats the back of a spoon, about 2 minutes. Remove from the heat and keep warm until ready to use.

To serve, transfer the potatoes to a serving dish and top with the pan sauce. Drizzle with the aioli, garnish with parsley and serve on its own or as a part of the Spanish Tapas Board (page 115).

SAFFRON AIOLI
1 tbsp (15 ml) fresh lemon juice

¼ tsp saffron threads

½ cup (115 g) mayonnaise

2 tbsp (30 ml) extra virgin olive oil

3 cloves garlic, minced

PATATAS BRAVAS
Extra-virgin olive oil, for frying

2 lbs (905 g) new red potatoes, cut into 2" (5-cm) chunks

1 tbsp (8 g) all-purpose flour

2 tbsp (30 ml) tomato paste

1 tsp smoked paprika

1 tsp paprika

1 cup (240 ml) beef stock

1 tsp chopped fresh parsley

PART IV

CLOSE-TO-HOME FAVORITES

Many of my recipes are inspired by my travels and personal experiences around North America. One needs to get out of one's "bubble" sometimes. And you don't have to travel outside the United States or even your immediate locale to find inspiration. I live in Southern California, but when I travel to different parts of the state, I find new and different cuisines. Traveling to, and enjoying food in, different sections of the United States has also stimulated my creativity and provided me with the inspiration for some of my boards. A visit to Hawaii provided a whole new food experience that inspired a board perfect for summer gatherings around the pool under the hot sun (page 137). Make the Mexican-Inspired Board (page 147) to kick off your next family taco night; the Southern-Inspired Board (page 125) makes a delicious appetizer for homemade barbecue.

SOUTHERN-INSPIRED BOARD

SERVES 10 TO 12

Green Tomato Chutney (page 129)

Boudin Balls with Cajun Aioli
(page 130)

1 loaf sourdough bread, cut into 1"
(2.5-cm) chunks

Classic Southern Pimento Cheese
(page 134)

1 bunch small carrots, peeled

1 bunch small red radishes

2 tbsp (30 ml) whole-grain Dijon
mustard

¼ cup (80 g) red pepper jelly

8 oz (225 g) smoked deli ham

4 oz (115 g) okra, halved lengthwise

3 medium heads endive, leaves
separated

½ cup (71 g) cornichons

½ cup (50 g) halved pecans

2 medium peaches, pitted and
sliced

1 (4-oz [115-g]) box saltine crackers

While I was growing up, our house was the one where everyone would come to hang out. Any given night of the week, we could have up to ten people for dinner, which was a big step up from my four-person immediate family. Both my brother's friends and mine became family, and we loved having barbecues by the pool in the summer or unexpected pasta dinners in the winter. Although I didn't grow up in the South, I have adopted the concept of "southern hospitality" and love being the hostess. Numerous trips down past the Mason-Dixon Line through southern states introduced me to the wonder of southern food. I love the influence from so many different cultures, the combination of high and low ingredients and the punches of spice and flavor that permeate southern cuisine.

This board is filled with a variety of textures from the crispy Boudin Balls with Cajun Aioli (page 130), sweet and tangy Green Tomato Chutney (page 129) and smooth and creamy Classic Southern Pimento Cheese (page 134). These elements are accompanied by various southern-grown favorites for pairing, such as okra and peaches.

EARLIER IN THE WEEK
Purchase all the ingredients needed for the board. Prepare the Green Tomato Chutney (can be made up to 2 weeks in advance) and store it refrigerated until ready to use. Marinate and make the pork for the Boudin Balls with Cajun Aioli, and kept it refrigerated. Cut the bread and store it in resealable bags.

1 DAY BEFORE SERVING
Make the Classic Southern Pimento Cheese and store it refrigerated in an airtight container. Make the boudin ball mixture and its Cajun aioli, then cover and refrigerate until ready to use.

Slice the carrots into halves, place them in a resealable plastic bag and refrigerate until ready to use. Halve the radishes, place them in a bowl of ice water and refrigerate to keep crisp.

(Continued)

SOUTHERN-INSPIRED BOARD (CONTINUED)

1 HOUR BEFORE SERVING

Prepare and fry the boudin balls, then arrange them on one side of a large board or platter. Place the Cajun aioli in a small bowl next to the boudin balls. Place the chutney and pimento cheese in individual bowls and arrange them on opposite sides of the board so the board looks balanced, using the photo as a guide for placement, if you'd like. Place the Dijon and red pepper jelly in individual small condiment bowls and place them around the board so they aren't too clumped together. Roll the deli ham so it's more visually appealing and arrange it on the board, filling in the spaces with the radishes, carrots, okra, endive, cornichons, pecans and peaches. Fill in the final spaces with the bread and saltine crackers.

GREEN TOMATO CHUTNEY

MAKES 2 (8-OUNCE [240-ML]) JARS

This versatile chutney can be used to top crackers, as an accoutrement on the Southern-Inspired Board (page 125), on sandwiches or as a topping on fried chicken or pork chops. Although green tomatoes will ripen over time if left on the kitchen counter, I like to take advantage of their unripe qualities. Green tomatoes are firm, crisp and sour (think: Granny Smith apples). They are great for chutney because they hold their form when cooked, thereby adding texture. Since this recipe makes a fairly large amount, I like to give one jar as a unique hostess gift!

8 medium firm green tomatoes

1 medium yellow onion

½ cup (75 g) golden raisins

1 cup (200 g) granulated sugar

⅔ cup (160 ml) white vinegar

2 tsp (2 g) crushed red pepper flakes

1 tsp yellow mustard seeds

1 tsp fennel seeds

1 tsp kosher salt

Core and dice the tomatoes and place them in a medium saucepan along with the onion, raisins, sugar, vinegar, red pepper flakes and mustard and fennel seeds. Bring to a simmer over medium heat and cook, stirring occasionally, until the mixture develops a jam-like consistency, about 1 hour. Season with the salt.

Ladle the mixture into two sterilized 8-ounce (240-ml) Mason jars. Refrigerate until ready to use. The chutney can be made up to 2 weeks ahead of time. Serve spread on crackers or with the Southern-Inspired Board (page 125).

BOUDIN BALLS WITH CAJUN AIOLI

MAKES ABOUT 35 BOUDIN BALLS

Traditional Cajun boudin sausage is made from a mixture of pork and chicken liver with the "Cajun holy trinity" of celery, onion and bell pepper, and seasoned with Cajun spices. Here it forgoes the process of casing and is instead rolled into balls, coated in a panko bread crumb coating and then fried. The appetizer is served with a quick, spiced aioli. Rather than making an aioli from scratch, I whisk olive oil, garlic and Cajun spices into mayonnaise to dress it up. Although this recipe includes directions for homemade boudin sausage, you might not have time to mix the sausage ingredients. If this is the case, substitute 2½ pounds (1.1 kg) of premade boudin sausage with the casings removed and proceed from making the egg wash. The crispy balls of pork sausage are the perfect contrast of texture when served with the other elements on the Southern-Inspired Board (page 125), such as the creamy Classic Southern Pimento Cheese (page 134). Try adding a bit of the board's red pepper jelly to the bites!

Prepare the boudin: In a medium bowl, combine the pork, liver, celery, bell pepper, onion and jalapeños, cover and refrigerate to marinate for at least 1 hour or overnight. Transfer the meat mixture to a large pot and cover with water. Bring the mixture to a boil over medium-high heat, then lower the heat to medium-low and simmer until fork-tender, about 2 hours.

Remove from the heat and drain. Stir in the pork fat, then cover and refrigerate for at least 1 hour and up to overnight. Process the solids through a meat grinder set to a coarse grind (you can also finely chop them with a knife, if you don't have a meat grinder).

Place the mixture in a large bowl, stir in the rice, parsley, green onion and cayenne, then season with salt and pepper. Stir in 1 of the eggs so the mixture holds together. Form the mixture into 1½-inch (4-cm) balls. At this point, the balls can be frozen until ready to use, for up to 1 month.

(Continued)

BOUDIN

1½ lbs (680 g) pork shoulder, cut into 1" (2.5-cm) chunks

4 oz (115 g) chicken liver, cut into 1" (2.5-cm) chunks

1 rib celery, chopped

1 medium green bell pepper, cored, seeded and diced

½ medium yellow onion, diced

3 medium jalapeño peppers, seeds and ribs removed, diced

¼ cup (42 g) pork fat

2½ cups (465 g) cooked white rice

¼ cup (15 g) chopped fresh flat-leaf parsley

⅓ cup (32 g) thinly sliced green onion

1 tsp cayenne pepper

Kosher salt and freshly ground black pepper

5 large eggs, divided

1 cup (240 ml) whole milk

3 cups (180 g) panko bread crumbs

Vegetable oil, for frying

CAJUN AIOLI

1 cup (225 g) mayonnaise

¼ cup (60 ml) extra virgin olive oil

3 cloves garlic, minced

1 tsp paprika

1 tsp onion powder

½ tsp dried oregano

½ tsp dried thyme

½ tsp cayenne pepper

BOUDIN BALLS WITH CAJUN AIOLI (CONTINUED)

When ready to fry the boudin balls, whisk together the remaining 4 eggs and the milk in a medium bowl. Place the panko in a shallow bowl and set aside. Working 1 ball at a time, dip the boudin balls into the egg wash, then into the panko mixture. Pour enough oil into a large cast-iron pan to reach 1 inch (2.5 cm) up the sides of the pan and heat to 350°F (177°C). Working a few at a time, add the balls and fry until deep golden brown all over, about 4 minutes. Transfer to a paper towel–lined plate to drain.

Prepare the Cajun aioli: In a small bowl, whisk together all the aioli ingredients. Cover and refrigerate until ready to use. The aioli can be made up to a week ahead of time. Serve the balls on their own or on the Southern-Inspired Board (page 125) with the aioli for dipping.

CLASSIC SOUTHERN PIMENTO CHEESE

SERVES 6 TO 8

Pimento cheese, a southern staple, is actually not a type of cheese; it's a cheese dip or spread similar to pub cheese. It's made from a combination of cream cheese, mayonnaise, cheese and sweet, jarred pimiento peppers. While every host or hostess has his or her own version, this is my tried-and-true recipe. When I first started going to football games in Alabama, southerners were appalled to find I had never had pimento cheese! It's considered the "pâté of the South"; southerners eat it on everything from sandwiches to slathered saltine crackers and vegetables. Here, it is a feature of the Southern-Inspired Board (page 125).

8 oz (225 g) cream cheese, at room temperature

¼ cup (60 g) mayonnaise

1 tsp Tabasco or hot sauce of choice

1 tsp Dijon mustard

¼ tsp cayenne pepper

¼ tsp smoked paprika

1½ cups (173 g) shredded sharp Cheddar cheese

1 (4-oz [113-g]) jar pimiento peppers, drained and chopped

2 tbsp (18 g) diced dill pickle

1 medium green onion, thinly sliced

In a medium bowl, stir together the cream cheese, mayonnaise, Tabasco, mustard, cayenne and paprika with a wooden spoon until combined. Add the cheddar, pimientos and pickle, continuing to stir until combined but slightly chunky. Refrigerate in an airtight container until ready to use.

This mixture can be made up to a week ahead of time. Top with the green onion. Serve with the Southern-Inspired Board (page 125) or with crackers and vegetables.

HAWAIIAN PUPU PLATTER

Kalua Pork Pan-Fried Dumplings
(page 138)

Wonton-Wrapped Fried Shrimp
with Sweet and Spicy Guava Sauce
(page 142)

Mini Spicy Ahi Poke Cups in Butter
Lettuce (page 145)

1 medium pineapple, peeled, cored
and cut into 1½" (4-cm) chunks

¼ cup (60 ml) soy sauce

2 tbsp (30 ml) sriracha

7 oz (200 g) dried mango slices

1 (0.5-oz [14-g]) package roasted
nori seaweed snacks

½ cup (73 g) roasted and salted
peanuts

¾ cup (101 g) roasted and salted
macadamia nuts

1 (7.5-oz [213-g]) bag Maui onion
chips or onion-flavored chips

2 medium passion fruit, halved

3 medium guava, halved

No matter where you live, this platter aims to take you to the lush tropical locale of the Hawaiian Islands. This board combines spins on some of Hawaii's greatest foods with multicultural influence, such as guava shrimp (page 142) and poke (page 145), with popular exports, such as macadamia nuts, and fresh fruit, such as guava and pineapple, for a platter inspired by the islands. Hawaii is a popular vacation destination from California, about a five-hour flight, and due to its proximity, many of the dishes have spread to the mainland. The most popular these days is poke—with iterations and spins on this Hawaiian raw fish dish being sold all over the United States. On a recent trip to Oahu, I got to expand my knowledge of the local cuisine—research that included several trips around the island for malasadas, garlicky shrimp, shave ice and white sandy beaches.

EARLIER IN THE WEEK

Purchase all the ingredients needed for the board. Make the pork mixture for the Kalua Pork Pan-Fried Dumplings, assemble the dumplings and freeze until ready to fry. Make the sauce for the Wonton-Wrapped Fried Shrimp with Sweet and Spicy Guava Sauce and refrigerate it in an airtight container until ready to use.

1 DAY BEFORE SERVING

Make the poke for the Mini Spicy Ahi Poke Cups in Butter Lettuce (but do not plate on the butter lettuce yet). Cover and refrigerate until ready to use. Peel or thaw the shrimp, if necessary, and store them refrigerated in resealable plastic bags. Cut the pineapple and store it refrigerated in an airtight container until ready to use.

1 HOUR BEFORE SERVING

Remove the dumplings from the freezer and fry the pork dumplings. Fry the wonton-wrapped shrimp and set aside, covered, until ready to serve. Plate the poke mixture on its butter lettuce cups.

Arrange the shrimp, dumplings and poke cups on a large board or platter, using the photo as a guide, if you'd like. Place the guava sauce for the shrimp in a small bowl, place the soy sauce and sriracha for dipping the dumplings in another small bowl and arrange them both on the platter. Fill in the spaces with the pineapple, mango, nori snacks, nuts and Maui onion chips, followed by the colorful passion fruit and guava.

KALUA PORK PAN-FRIED DUMPLINGS

MAKES ABOUT 40 DUMPLINGS

Although traditional kalua pork is made by wrapping the pork in banana leaves, this is a more approachable, at-home version whereby the pork is slowly cooked at a low temperature with a few simple ingredients, including liquid smoke, to retain that classic smoky flavor. The tender pork is shredded and used as stuffing for pan-fried dumplings. Since kalua pork is a staple at luaus, it is a natural fit on the Hawaiian Pupu Platter (page 137). This recipe is great because the assembled dumplings can be made ahead of time and frozen, then taken out when ready to use. As the meat is already cooked, it only takes a few minutes to heat and serve!

Prepare the kalua pork: Preheat the oven to 325°F (165°C). Oil a medium Dutch oven or heavy-bottomed pot with a lid with the oil and heat over medium heat. Season the pork all over with the salt, then add it to the pot and sear until golden brown on all sides, about 6 minutes total. Add the chicken stock and liquid smoke and bring the mixture to a boil, then cover the pot. Transfer the Dutch oven to the oven and cook until the pork is fork-tender, 2 to 2½ hours.

Remove from the oven, remove the pork from the pot and let cool, then shred the meat and set it aside with 2 tablespoons (30 ml) of the cooking liquid until ready to use. The pork can be made ahead and kept refrigerated in an airtight container for up to 2 days (the dumplings are easier to fill if the mixture is cool).

Prepare the dumplings: In a large bowl, mix together the shredded pork, ginger, garlic, green onions, cabbage and eggs until thoroughly combined.

(continued)

KALUA PORK
1 tbsp (15 ml) vegetable oil

2½ lbs (1.1 kg) boneless pork butt, with fat cap

2 tsp (13 g) coarse Himalayan pink salt

1 cup (240 ml) chicken stock

1 tsp liquid smoke

DUMPLINGS
1 tbsp (6 g) minced fresh ginger

2 cloves garlic, minced

2 green onions, thinly sliced

1 cup (90 g) shredded green cabbage

2 large eggs, lightly beaten

1 (10-oz [280-g]) package round gyoza wrappers

KALUA PORK PAN-FRIED DUMPLINGS (CONTINUED)

To assemble the dumplings, place 1 dumpling wrapper on a clean surface. Keep the remaining wrappers covered with a damp cloth so they do not dry out. Spoon 1 tablespoon (16 g) of the filling into the middle of the wrapper. Fold the wrapper in half so that it forms a half-moon shape. Starting on one end, pinch the wrapper tightly together, repeating until the dumpling is completely sealed. Stand the dumpling, seam side up, on a parchment paper–lined baking sheet. Continue with the remaining filling and dumpling wrappers. At this point, the dumplings can either be frozen in plastic bags or cooked.

To serve, once all of the dumplings are formed, place a large sauté pan with a lid over medium heat, add the vegetable oil and heat through. Working in batches, arrange the dumplings in the pan in a tight circular pattern standing up in the oil, seam side up. Cook, uncovered, until the bottoms of the dumplings are golden brown, about 2 minutes.

Add ¼ cup (60 ml) of water to the pan, then cover tightly with the lid (do this quickly, as the liquid will splatter) and cook until most of the liquid has been absorbed and the bottoms of the dumplings are crisp and golden, about 5 minutes. Remove the dumplings from the pan with tongs and place them on a paper towel–lined plate. Serve hot on the Hawaiian Pupu Platter (page 137) or on their own with a side of soy sauce and sriracha.

TIP: **Try dipping the dumplings in the Sweet and Spicy Guava Sauce from page 142.**

TO SERVE
3 tbsp (45 ml) vegetable oil

WONTON-WRAPPED FRIED SHRIMP WITH SWEET AND SPICY GUAVA SAUCE

SERVES 6

The famed shrimp trucks on the shores of Oahu, Hawaii, inspired this version of fried shrimp. At Romy's Shrimp Stand, wonton-wrapped fried shrimp is offered in addition to classic garlic butter shrimp. I use egg roll wrappers for these fried shrimp because they are slightly bigger than the wonton wrappers sold in stores and are easy to wrap when halved diagonally. The tail sticking out of the end of the wrapper makes for an impressive presentation, not to mention easy eating! As one of Hawaii's biggest exports, shrimp pair perfectly with the other fresh elements on the Hawaiian Pupu Platter (page 137) and their crispiness contrasts with the Mini Spicy Ahi Poke Cups in Butter Lettuce (page 145) and the Kalua Pork Pan-Fried Dumplings (page 138).

Prepare the guava sauce: In a small saucepan, whisk together the guava jam, lime juice, sugar and chili paste over medium heat until the sugar has dissolved, about 5 minutes. Remove from the heat and set aside.

Refrigerate in an airtight container until ready to use. The sauce can be made up to a week ahead of time and served at room temperature.

Prepare the fried shrimp: Season the shrimp with salt and pepper. Working one shrimp at a time, lay the shrimp in the center of an egg roll wrapper, leaving the tail out at the top (the straight side). Bring the pointed edge of the wrapper tightly over the shrimp, folding in one side and rolling until completely wrapped. Fill a small bowl with water, then dip a finger or brush in the water, rub the water on the edge of the wonton wrapper and press to seal the wrapper shut. Set aside on a parchment paper–lined baking sheet and repeat with the remaining wonton wrappers and shrimp.

Heat enough vegetable oil in a heavy-bottomed pot or Dutch oven to reach 1½ inches (4 cm) up the side and heat over medium heat until the oil reaches 350°F (177°C). Working in batches, add the wrapped shrimp to the oil and fry until golden brown, about 2 minutes per side. Transfer to a paper towel–lined plate to drain and repeat with the remaining wrapped shrimp.

Serve with the guava sauce on the Hawaiian Pupu Platter (page 137) or on their own.

SWEET AND SPICY GUAVA SAUCE

½ cup (160 g) guava jam

2 tbsp (30 ml) fresh lime juice

2 tbsp (26 g) granulated sugar

2 tbsp (30 ml) sambal chili paste

WONTON-WRAPPED FRIED SHRIMP

1½ lbs (680 g) colossal (U/15) shrimp, peeled and deveined, tails on

Kosher salt and freshly ground black pepper

1 lb (455 g) egg roll wrappers, halved diagonally

Vegetable oil, for frying

MINI SPICY AHI POKE CUPS IN BUTTER LETTUCE

SERVES 8

I love any type of raw fish, but poke has been a staple for me the past few years as it has gained popularity in the mainland United States and not just Hawaii. Ahi tuna is the most classic and authentic version of poke; however, I have seen it made many different ways using everything from salmon to octopus. If you want to mix it up a bit, the ahi in this recipe can be subbed out for another fish or seafood, like salmon or yellowtail. For those skeptical of raw fish, I recommend using chopped, cooked shrimp instead. In this recipe, the fish is served tossed in a spicy shoyu sauce. I love the contrast of the fresh raw fish in this recipe paired with the Wonton-Wrapped Fried Shrimp (page 142) on the Hawaiian Pupu Platter (page 137).

The poke can be made a day ahead of time and scooped into the butter lettuce serving cups just prior to serving. Since high-quality, sushi-grade raw fish can be expensive, such additions as edamame or avocado can be added to stretch the recipe further.

In a medium bowl, whisk together the sesame oil, soy sauce, sriracha and rice vinegar. Fold in the tuna, onion, green onion and sesame seeds until combined. Add the edamame and avocado (if using). Cover and refrigerate until ready to use. The poke can be made up to 1 day in advance.

When ready to serve, let the poke sit at room temperature for 15 to 20 minutes, then scoop the mixture into the butter lettuce cups. Serve on the Hawaiian Pupu Platter (page 137) or on their own.

TIP: The ahi tuna will be consumed raw, so it is important to purchase sushi-grade fish for the recipe. The fish is flash-frozen to kill any potentially harmful parasites, making it safe for consumption while maintaining quality.

3 tbsp (45 ml) toasted sesame oil

2 tbsp (30 ml) soy sauce

2 tbsp (30 ml) sriracha

1 tbsp (15 ml) rice vinegar

1 lb (455 g) sushi-grade ahi tuna, diced into ½" (1.3-cm) cubes

¼ cup (40 g) thinly sliced sweet yellow onion

2 tbsp (12 g) thinly sliced green onion

2 tsp (6 g) black and white sesame seeds

½ cup (78 g) shelled edamame (optional)

1 medium Hass avocado, pitted, peeled and chopped (optional)

2 large heads butter lettuce, leaves separated

MEXICAN-INSPIRED BOARD

SERVES 10 TO 12

Grilled Peach and Orange Salsa (page 148)

Shrimp Ceviche (page 151)

Guacamole with Charred Corn (page 152)

1 medium jicama, peeled and cut into sticks

3 medium assorted color bell peppers, cored, seeded and sliced

4 medium carrots, peeled and cut into sticks

1 bunch red radishes, halved

10 oz (280 g) prepared queso fresco

1 cup (150 g) cherry tomatoes

12 oz (340 g) sliced, pickled jalapeño peppers, drained

½ cup (70 g) roasted and salted pumpkin seeds

1 (13-oz [369-g]) bag tortilla chips

1 (5-oz [142-g]) bag plantain chips

Lime wedges, for garnish

Fresh cilantro leaves, for garnish

Living in Southern California has taught me so much about Mexican cuisine. One of my favorite things is the layers of deep flavor within every dish. From spices like chiles (both fresh and roasted), cilantro and cumin to bright zesty notes of lime, creamy avocado and crisp corn, there are so many different textures and flavor profiles that work in harmony for delectable dishes. So many of the fresh ingredients that make Mexican food so great are found right here in Southern California. You can't attend a party here without a big bowl of guacamole and salsa! I love serving twists on the traditional staples along with plenty of colorful vegetables for dipping.

In this board, an assortment of my takes on Mexican appetizers, such as Grilled Peach and Orange Salsa (page 148), Guacamole with Charred Corn (page 152) and Shrimp Ceviche (page 151) are served alongside crumbly cheeses, such as queso fresco, and an assortment of vegetables fit for any fiesta. This spread is best paired with a margarita (homemade only; no sugary mixes for me) or an ice-cold beer.

EARLIER IN THE WEEK
Purchase all the ingredients needed for the board. Make the Grilled Peach and Orange Salsa and store it refrigerated in an airtight container.

1 DAY BEFORE SERVING
Make the Shrimp Ceviche and store it refrigerated in an airtight container until ready to use. Char the corn for the Guacamole with Charred Corn in advance and store it refrigerated in an airtight container. Cut the jicama, peppers and carrots and store them refrigerated in resealable plastic bags. Cut the radishes, place them in a bowl of ice water and refrigerate them to keep them crisp.

1 HOUR BEFORE SERVING
Prepare the guacamole recipe. Place the guacamole, salsa and ceviche in individual serving bowls and arrange them in different areas of the board, using the photo as a guide, if you'd like. Position the queso fresco in another area of the board and fill in the rest of the board with the tomatoes, jicama, peppers, carrots, radishes, pickled jalapeños and pumpkin seeds. Serve with the tortilla chips and plantain chips. Garnish with lime wedges and cilantro leaves.

GRILLED PEACH AND ORANGE SALSA

MAKES ABOUT 2 CUPS (250 G) OF SALSA

Grilling peaches gives them a rich flavor and brings out their natural sweetness, allowing them to hold up to the spicy flavors of the jalapeños and fresh cilantro in this tasty salsa. The orange juice complements the vibrant flavors of the peaches. Summer is the best time to make this salsa, when stone fruits are at their peak. Look for peaches that are fairly firm but have a little give, particularly around the stem—they'll continue to get sweeter and juicer as they ripen. This flavorful fruit-based twist on salsa is the perfect contrast to the creamy, mellow Guacamole with Charred Corn (page 152) for a great dip duo on the Mexican-Inspired Board (page 147).

4 medium yellow peaches, halved and pitted

2 tbsp (30 ml) vegetable oil

1 medium yellow onion, diced

2 medium jalapeño peppers, seeds and ribs removed, diced

¼ cup (60 ml) fresh orange juice

2 tbsp (30 ml) fresh lime juice

¼ cup (10 g) chopped fresh cilantro

Kosher salt

Prepare a gas or charcoal grill to direct medium heat. Brush the peaches with the oil and arrange, cut side down, on the grill grates. Cook, uncovered, until grill marks appear, about 5 minutes. Flip the peaches and cook, uncovered, until tender, about an additional 4 minutes.

Roughly chop the peaches. In a food processor fitted with a blade attachment or blender, combine the peaches, onion, jalapeños, orange juice, lime juice and cilantro and pulse the salsa a few times so that it is still slightly chunky but more of a puree. Season to taste with salt.

Transfer to an airtight container and refrigerate until ready to serve. This salsa can be made up to 1 week in advance. Serve with the Mexican-Inspired Board (page 147) or on its own with tortilla chips.

SHRIMP CEVICHE

SERVES 6

Traditional ceviche is made by marinating fish or shellfish in citrus juice. The acid from the citrus essentially "cooks" the raw ingredient and gives it a bright flavor. Ceviche makes for a perfect appetizer featuring a protein, but without turning on the oven, so the zesty dish is perfect for hot summer days in addition to the Guacamole with Charred Corn (page 152) and Grilled Peach and Orange Salsa (page 148) from the Mexican-Inspired Board (page 147). One of my favorite types of ceviche is made with shrimp combined with juicy tomatoes and creamy avocado, which complement the blend of citrus. This recipe is best made just before serving but comes together with very minimal work.

Chop the shrimp into ½-inch (1.3-cm) pieces and place them in a medium bowl. Toss with the lemon, lime and orange juice, red onion and serrano peppers until combined. Cover and refrigerate, stirring occasionally, until the shrimp firms up slightly and is no longer opaque, about 45 minutes.

Just prior to serving, toss together with the tomatoes, cilantro and avocado and season to taste with salt. Serve on the Mexican-Inspired Board (page 147) or with tortilla chips.

1 lb (455 g) extra-large (26/30) shrimp, peeled and deveined, tails removed

¼ cup (60 ml) fresh lemon juice

¼ cup (60 ml) fresh lime juice

2 tbsp (30 ml) fresh orange juice

¼ cup (40 g) diced red onion

2 serrano peppers, seeds and ribs removed, finely diced

¾ cup (113 g) halved cherry tomatoes

¼ cup (10 g) chopped fresh cilantro

1 medium Hass avocado, pitted, peeled and chopped

Kosher salt

GUACAMOLE WITH CHARRED CORN

SERVES 6

In my take on classic guacamole, mashing the avocados with onion, serrano peppers, cilantro and lime juice allows the flavors to blend into the mixture. Adding charred corn to the guacamole creates a contrast in texture to the smooth avocados. The key to a great guacamole is to use ripe avocados—when buying avocados, give them a gentle squeeze in the palm of your hand; they should be firm but give slightly. If you are planning ahead for this recipe, buy a very firm avocado so that it ripens by the end of the week. On the other hand, if you need to ripen a hard avocado quickly, place it in a paper bag and close the bag loosely, letting it sit overnight. When serving guacamole, don't limit yourself to just eating it with tortilla chips; take a note from the Mexican-Inspired Board (page 147) and try pairing it with crisp vegetables, such as jicama.

2 ears of corn, husks removed

2 tbsp (30 ml) vegetable oil

6 medium Hass avocados, halved and pitted

½ medium red onion, minced

2 serrano peppers, seeds and ribs removed, minced

¼ cup (10 g) packed chopped fresh cilantro

2 tbsp (30 ml) fresh lime juice

Kosher salt

Heat a grill to medium-high heat. Brush the ears of corn with the oil and place them on the grill. Cook until slightly charred on all sides, 4 to 6 minutes. Remove from the grill and let cool completely.

Scoop the avocado flesh into a medium bowl and add the red onion, peppers, cilantro and lime juice. Mash, using a potato masher, the back of a fork or a rubber spatula, until the avocado is smooth. Cut the kernels off the corn cobs and fold them into the guacamole until they are evenly incorporated. Season to taste with salt.

The guacamole can be made 1 day ahead of time, covered with plastic wrap and refrigerated until ready to use, but is best when made fresh so it doesn't brown. If refrigerating for any period of time, squeeze a little bit of lime juice over the top and push the plastic wrap right down on top of the guacamole so there is as little air in the container as possible. Serve on the Mexican-Inspired Board (page 147) or with tortilla chips or crisp vegetables.

ACKNOWLEDGMENTS

Thank you Aaron—you keep me going day after day. You've eaten every single thing in this book and continue to be my sounding board, my partner and best friend. Thank you for encouraging me to share my recipes with the world. I love you.

Thank you Mom, Dad and Josh for always inspiring me and pushing me to follow my dreams. I don't know what I would do without your constant and unwavering support (and recipe testing); it means the world to me.

Thank you to Nana and Papa, for always dealing with my grammar and constant need for editing. Thank you for waking up early on the East Coast to look over my recipes before I need them when I start my day on the West Coast.

Thank you to Dannette, Paul, Katie and Annie, who have always treated me like one of their own.

Thank you to all of my incredible friends and family who took the time to test recipes included in this book, send photos, help me stay organized and sane, grocery shop and hand model. I am forever thankful to be surrounded by such incredible people I can always rely on. My boys Pat, Mark and David. Devin, Paige, Kurt, Bill, Patricia, Elexa, Ian, Cory, Jim, Jillian, Ben, Kirsten, Alex, Jamie, Zoey, Oliva, Sophia, Erika, Demi, Raj, Alana, Leslie, Jeetu, Sean, Scott, Natalie, Tess, April, Monica, Sophia, Danielle, Galal, Grace, Ryan, James, Rhodes, Pat, Patty, Ross, Dylan, Amelie, Octavia, EB, Celena, Amy, Sydney, Erin, Carrie, Booth, Jess, Brian, Rachel, Mallory, Rebecca, Luann, my locals, my bookworms and my neighbors. There are too many of you to count and I am so lucky.

Thank you Sarah, my marvelous editor, for encouraging me to write this book and seeing me through the crazy process. You make me work harder and smarter. I was new to the world of developing a book and I am so grateful that you patiently worked with me, never letting me down. Thank you to everyone at Page Street Publishing for believing in me and my vision.

Last but certainly not least, thank you to all the loyal followers of Cooking with Cocktail Rings who have helped me achieve this life-long goal and who continue to make this all possible. I do this all for you!

xx,

Kylie

ABOUT THE AUTHOR

Kylie is the author/cook/photographer behind the blog Cooking with Cocktail Rings, inspiring others to cook restaurant-quality dishes in their own kitchens. Since starting her site, her work has been featured on BuzzFeed, Better Homes & Gardens and Eater, among others. Kylie lives in Santa Monica, California, where she creates recipes in her cozy apartment kitchen and can typically be found working on the couch alongside her cat, Stella. This is her debut cookbook.

INDEX